WELSH
SPORTING
GREATS

WELSH
SPORTING
GREATS

Edited by
ALUN WYN BEVAN

First Impression—2001

ISBN 1 85902 892 6

Printed in Wales by
Gomer Press, Llandysul, Ceredigion

'Sport has the power to change the world, the power to inspire, the power to unite people in a way that little else can.'

Nelson Mandela

'Just don't get too down when you're down and don't get too high when you're high.'

Australian cricket captain Steve Waugh to his wicketkeeper
Adam Gilchrist

'I was never coached; I was never told how to hold a bat.'

Sir Donald Bradman (1908 - 2001)

'I can accept failure. Everyone fails at something. But I can't accept not trying.'

Michael Jordan

'I started in a college, failed to complete the course. And then after deciding to concentrate on my interests I received six doctorates from the world's foremost universities.'

Sir Edmund Hillary

'Perfection is impossible, but in the pursuit of perfection we can achieve excellence.'

Anon

CONTENTS

JAMES ALFORD	1	TERRY GRIFFITHS	56
IVOR ALLCHURCH	2	CHRIS HALLAM	58
W. J. BANCROFT	4	JUDGE ROWE HARDING	59
GERALD BATTRICK	5	ROBERT HOWLEY	60
JAMIE BAULCH	6	BRIAN HUGGETT	62
PHIL BENNETT	8	MARK HUGHES	63
JOHN C. BEVAN	9	COLIN JACKSON	65
BILLY BOSTON	11	STEVE JAMES	66
DAVID BROOME	12	ALBERT JENKINS	68
JOE CALZAGHE	15	NEIL JENKINS	69
JOHN CHARLES	16	BARRY JOHN	71
ROBERT CROFT	18	ALAN JONES	73
BRIAN CURVIS	20	BRYN JONES	74
GERALD DAVIES	21	CLIFF JONES	75
HYWEL DAVIES	23	CLIFF JONES	76
JONATHAN DAVIES	24	COLIN JONES	78
LYNN DAVIES	26	D. K. JONES	79
MERVYN DAVIES	28	ERIC JONES	81
MICHAEL DAVIES	29	JEFF JONES	82
TERRY DAVIES	31	JONATHAN JONES	84
VALERIE DAVIES	32	KEN JONES	85
JOHN DISLEY	33	LEWIS JONES	87
DAI DOWER	35	LOUISE JONES	88
JIM DRISCOLL	36	PERCY JONES	90
GARETH EDWARDS	37	ROBERT JONES	91
HUGH EDWARDS	38	STEVE JONES	94
ANNE ELLIS	40	FRED KEENOR	95
JOE ERSKINE	41	JACK KELSEY	96
SIR CHARLES EVANS	42	TONY LEWIS	97
EDGAR EVANS	44	CARL LLEWELLYN	98
GWYNDAF EVANS	45	HARRY LLEWELLYN	100
IEUAN EVANS	46	MATTHEW MAYNARD	102
MALDWYN LEWIS EVANS	48	BILLY MEREDITH	104
TOMMY FARR	49	B. V. MEREDITH	105
TREVOR FORD	51	JOHN MERRIMAN	107
SCOTT GIBBS	53	CLIFF MORGAN	108
RYAN GIGGS	54	DAVID MORGAN	110

HYWEL MORGAN	111	IWAN THOMAS	144
KELLY MORGAN	112	JOHN GREGORY THOMAS	146
HUGH MORRIS	114	PARRY THOMAS	147
GILBERT PARKHOUSE	115	TANNI GREY THOMPSON	149
BERWYN PRICE	116	MAURICE TURNBULL	150
GRAHAM PRICE	118	KIRSTY WADE	151
JOHN PRICE	119	NIGEL WALKER	152
TOM MALDWYN PRYCE	120	PETER WALKER	154
MARILYN PUGH	122	CYRIL WALTERS	155
SCOTT QUINNELL	124	STEVE WATKIN	156
PAUL RADMILOVIC	125	ALLAN WATKINS	159
KEVIN RATCLIFFE	126	DAVID WATKINS	160
RAY REARDON	127	FREDDIE WELSH	161
DAI REES	129	HELEN WESTON	163
LEIGHTON REES	130	JIMMY WILDE	164
DICK RICHARDSON	131	BLEDDYN WILLIAMS	165
SIAN ROBERTS	132	FREDDIE WILLIAMS	167
IAN RUSH	133	J. J. WILLIAMS	169
DON SHEPHERD	134	J. P. R. WILLIAMS	171
ALF SHERWOOD	135	MARK WILLIAMS	172
NEVILLE SOUTHALL	137	R. H. WILLIAMS	173
MATTHEW STEVENS	138	HOWARD WINSTONE	175
JIM SULLIVAN	140	MARTIN WOODROFFE	176
HAYDN TANNER	141	WILFRED WOOLLER	178
CLEM THOMAS	142	IAN WOOSNAM	179
DAVID THOMAS	143	TERRY YORATH	181

IN APPRECIATION

To all those who have contributed. Your willingness to share your recollections will brighten many a dark evening.

To the following for their assistance and support in obtaining photographs and text :

South Wales Evening Post, *South Wales Argus*, *Western Mail*, North Wales Newspapers, *Wigan Observer*, *Golwg*, *Barn*, Seat (UK), Welsh Sports Council, *The Times*, University of Wales Press, National Library of Wales, Cardiff Central Library, Newport Library, Press Association, John Harris, Gwydion Roberts, Audrey Woodroffe, Mark Lewis, Stewart Williams, Cathy Duncan, Paul Keenor, Diana Cook, Photo Gallery Wales, Steve Benbow at Photolibrary Wales, Jamie Battrick, Gwenda Lloyd Wallace, Ian Buchanan, Mark Shearman, John Hinton, Huw Evans Picture Agency, Photo Fiction, Andrew Gallymore, Jane Wyn, Owain Jones, Anthony Hughes, Mark Thomas, Anna Owen, Randall Isaac.

To Bethan Mair, Francesca Rhydderch and the publishers, Gomer Press at Llandysul, for their guidance, drive and enthusiasm throughout the past two years. To Bryn Terfel, a sporting enthusiast, for reminding us in the foreword that we've all been there in our dreams! Also to Donna Gray for designing the front cover. Any profits will be donated to charities.

And finally, to all those sporting superstars who didn't quite make it. Many apologies.

PREFACE

'It's John Hardy at the Racecourse with the quite remarkable news that Wales have just scored a second goal and are leading Italy by two goals to one in this vital World Cup qualifying fixture. Both Welsh goals scored by Bryn Terfel, from Manchester United, a former pupil at Ysgol Dyffryn Nantlle. The first came after fifteen minutes, an unstoppable volley into the roof of the net from twenty yards and the second a glancing header past Dino Zoff...'

When we are young we all dream of scaling the heights, of getting to the top in our chosen field. For those young Welshmen and women who are interested and dedicated to the arts, the goal is a place at the Royal Academy, the Guildhall or even RADA. This may lead to appearances on Broadway, the West End, the MET or the Royal Opera House.

I have been fortunate enough to have achieved one of my goals and performed at some of the world's great opera houses. But I have to admit that, as a youngster, it wasn't counting encores at La Scala which helped me sleep. Indeed it would have to have been that try I scored whilst representing Wales at Twickenham against the old enemy; the backhand volley which crushed John McEnroe in the final at Wimbledon or just pipping Carl Lewis on the line in the 200 metres final in the Olympics at Los Angeles in 1984. There was no end to my talents and those dreams were vivid and very real.

I can therefore only applaud those giants of the sporting world whose achievements have helped propel Wales to the forefront. I'm sure that, like me, as you browse through this book you will be fascinated by what you read of the stars of the past, puzzled as to how on earth so and so could possibly be included with the 'greats' and complain that 'you know who' should definitely merit a place.

With such lively discussion, there may even be, in true Hollywood tradition – a sequel!

Hwyl fawr,
Bryn Terfel

INTRODUCTION

Help! I'm fully aware that some of you might be considering putting pen to paper as a result of reading this particular volume – letters of protest to *The Western Mail, South Wales Evening Post, The Argus, The Daily Post, The Echo, The Wrexham Leader.* And the reason? Whilst browsing through the contents, some will realise that many icons haven't been included, geniuses completely overlooked. I hear the cry, 'Unforgivable.' How could the editor ignore great weightlifters, cyclists, athletes, snooker players etc…

Hundreds were considered; just over a hundred listed and the stars omitted substantial. How did he come to a decision? What criteria were implemented? Has he been fair to each sport?

During my years in Brynaman, several of us sport-mad youngsters spent a high percentage of our leisure hours on the village's cricket ground, a combination of the Arms Park, Lord's and Wembley! Adjacent to the lush green field was Mr Gwyn Howell's garden which also bordered with the lane that led to the ground. We all marvelled at the size of Mr Howell's onions even though the majority of us had no interest whatsoever in horticulture – Charlie Dimmocks were a rare breed in the sixties. We certainly appreciated the size, texture and composition of his onions. The devoted gardener regularly received cups and certificates at local and county Agricultural Shows. However, from time to time he arrived home feeling sorry for himself because the judges had favoured someone else's crop.

And that, to be blunt, is why some of your favourites have been ignored. For the purpose of this particular volume I just happened to be the sole judge and executioner. Eventually, decisions had to be made and thus I had to be clinical and ruthless. In the world of rugby I decided to favour those who had truly excelled whilst representing the British Lions. I would have liked to have included others; Brian Price, Delme Thomas, Alun Pask, Dewi Bebb, Terry Price, Maurice Richards, Ivor Jones, Bobby Windsor, Ray Gravell, John Davies, Keith Jarrett, Mark Ring. I would have liked to have written about one of the best centre three-quarters I ever saw, namely Cyril Davies. Sadly, as a result of injuries, his time as an international was cut short. And there were some truly outstanding individuals who represented Wales, the British Lions and the Barbarians whose devotion to their clubs in trying circumstances was to be commended. Elgan Rees was one such individual; Neath in dire straits, other clubs desperate for his services but Rees's loyalty an example to others.

Cricketers are absent – J. C. Clay, Willie Jones, Dai and Emrys Davies, Jim McConnon, Eifion Jones. Footballers such as Bob John, Wally Barnes, Ron Burgess, John Mahoney, Dean Saunders, Mike England, Ray Daniel, John

Toshack. And how on earth can I justify including those who came within a hair's breadth of succeeding whilst ignoring the claims of several champions? What about Tom Richards, Berwyn and Ron Jones, Robert Morgan, Leigh Jones, Kay Morley, Terry Sullivan, Steve Barry, Gwyn Nicholls, Dickie Owen, Jack Peterson, Tony Simmons, Nicky Piper, Robert Dickey, Johnny Owen, Alun Evans, Neil Winter, Pat Beavan, Mike Richards, Denis Reardon, Austin Savage and many others? And what about the current crop of young stars? There are no references to Richie Burnett, Steve Robinson, Hayley Tullet, Jayne Ludlow, Non Evans and Bethan Daunton.

To some readers, village outside-halves or centre-forwards from the past would have been Welsh Sporting Giants. I wrote to a relative from Clay Cross near Chesterfield (a football and cricket addict), asking him to write something on John Charles or Ian Rush or even Don Shepherd. He replied stating that his boyhood hero was Ronald William Herbert Powell, a Welshman who distinguished himself in goal for Chesterfield FC. David Cratchley's recollection is included below as a tribute to all those Welshmen and -women who've managed to provide many hours of pleasure for us sporting freaks.

When I received the letter from Alun to contribute an article on a famous Welsh sportsman, I was truly flattered, particularly when he casually mentioned the pedigree of some of the other contributors. I was somewhat dismayed however, when he explained quite clearly that he wanted a foreigner's viewpoint. Me – whose formative years were conditioned by a fiercely patriotic Welsh mother and many weeks spent in the Swansea Valley, always in the rain!

Several possible subjects were discussed, John Charles and Ian Rush amongst them. I soon realised that although I must have witnessed their skills against Chesterfield FC, Charles for Leeds United Reserves and Rush for Chester, I had never actually seen them play; they were on the wrong side. In fact I could contribute nothing more than tens of thousands of others with access to thirty or so volumes of Rothmans. Suddenly, the penny dropped. What about Ron Powell?

Robert William Herbert Powell was born in Knighton, and in his late teens he joined Manchester City, where for four years he proved a more than capable understudy for the finest keeper of his day, Frank Swift, deputising when the great man was on international duty or on the rare occasions when he was injured.

Ron Powell.

One can only imagine Powell's chagrin when on Swift's retirement his place was taken not by the sturdy youngster from mid-Wales but by a big blond German. Fortunately, in the early fifties, professional footballers did not throw their teddy-bears from the cot at the first sign of adversity; they carried on. In the summer of 1952, Ron decided to follow the well trodden path from Maine Road to Saltergate, the home of Chesterfield FC. This had been a fairly easy move for some others, such as inside forwards Tommy Capel and George Smith, as Chesterfield was never noted for its goal scorers. In contrast, Powell arrived to fill the goalmouth vacated only some twelve months previously by Ray Middleton, hero of Chesterfield and considered by most in the north of England to be second only to Swift, and by many in North Derbyshire to be the better of the two.

He was, however, more than equal to the challenge which he met with distinction for the next thirteen years. A model of consistency, in today's parlance an eight-out-of-ten player – rarely noticeably brilliant but after watching him for half a season one realised that he had never had a mediocre game. There were pretenders along the way, including a stripling from Sheffield by the name of Banks. However, he only lasted twenty or so games before moving on to a couple of Midlands clubs and seventy-three England caps. Powell's career was cruelly cut short in the 1964/65 season by a tragic car accident which also claimed the life of a team-mate Ralph Hunt during one of Chesterfield's better FA Cup runs, when we actually reached the third round. Who knows, if that accident had not occurred, would we have had to wait a further thirty-two years for our first semi-final appearance? That wonderful day at Old Trafford spoilt only by the incompetence of a school teacher from North London.

Although memories fade with age, two will remain for ever; one visual and one olfactory. Those of us who witnessed his performances every other Saturday will never forget the sight of his thighs straining the legs of his shorts nor his barrel chest straining the pale green well-washed polo neck sweater favoured by goalkeepers of those days. Nor will those of us who stood expectantly behind the goal forget the aroma of horse liniment as he threw his cloth cap into the net to prepare for the pre-match kick-in.

How then did Powell rate as a goalkeeper?

> *Competent*: obviously so; duck-eggs don't play almost five hundred league games.
>
> *Brave*: he had to be to share his working life with the likes of Dave Blakey, Jim Smallwood and the late lamented Tommy Flockett.
>
> *Athletic*: probably not; but any deficiency in this area was more than compensated for by his other attributes.

Behaviour: I cannot remember him being in trouble with referees, letting off even one fire extinguisher in an hotel or requiring an agent to explain some act of boorish behaviour.

I never had the courage to speak to Ron Powell, and sadly never will, following his untimely death in 1992. I therefore missed the chance to thank him and colleagues like him for giving me and so many of my generation the opportunity to develop an undying love for the game of soccer and a never-ending pride in my local team, which remains as strong as ever. These opportunities, I fear, will be denied to future generations.

Will future Ron Powells emerge? Probably not. At 5' 10" he would probably be six inches too short to warrant a second glance by some of today's Premiership scouts, and, in any event, would a Premiership goalkeeper be prepared to bridge the ever-increasing gulf to the Second Division?

Clubs such as Chesterfield relied heavily on the Ron Powells of this world and the ability to develop and transfer at a reasonable fee a star player after ten years, and a good player every three years. One cannot argue with the morality of the Bossman ruling, but unless action is taken the whole structure and nature of the sport will continue to change, and in my opinion for the worse.

Despite your protests, the axe had to fall and the intention, with the publisher's co-operation, is to prepare a second volume so that we can ensure a degree of fair play. That is certainly the intent.

Along with all the other contributors, to whom I am most grateful, I would have liked to have invited one more, one who would have added another dimension to the finished work. Friday morning in the seventies and early eighties amounted to real excitement and eager anticipation. At half past seven, *The Guardian* arrived – *The Manchester Guardian* not *The South Wales Guardian*! Over breakfast, an opportunity to digest Carwyn James's weekly article; an article which encapsulated perfectly everything in the world of rugby. About six hundred words as a rule, but I suspect he had been at it for hours, if not days, analysing, interpreting and speculating before inking his pen.

I'm grateful to John Evans from BBC Wales's Sports Department for agreeing to contribute the following short article on Carwyn.

Carwyn

Meeting him for the first time during January 1958. Our Welsh teacher, John Roderick Rees, who had not won the Eisteddfod crown at the time, happened to hear that we were going to Cardiff to watch the Australia match. 'If you see Carwyn,' he said jokingly, 'give him my regards. We were together in T. H. Parry Williams's class at university'.

If? We were determined to see him. We waited two hours before he stepped graciously, shyly, towards the hotel. Then the impudence of young boys demanding an autograph, passing on the message and insisting that we were now related. And even though he was representing his country for the first time in about two hours, he stopped and spoke to US! He was available to all, even at that time!

Ten years later I spent many hours in his company. Driving him, late usually, to games. The gatekeeper yelling, 'You don't have the right to come this way!' Then on seeing him, realising! 'Carwyn'. And the yell. 'Move everyone, Carwyn is here'. Using his first name only.

Sharing a small office with him with one easy chair in scruffy leather and full of small holes – evidence of his cigarettes. There he would be, half sleeping after an uncomfortable night because of an irritable skin complaint. The greats and the not so greats of the world on the telephone endlessly, with each one receiving the same courtesy and attention.

Sharing a commentary with Carwyn and Wales winning four triple crowns in succession. 'Following Gamaliel!' Sharing the snooker table occasionally, the only time I felt his equal. Exchanging ceremonies; serious rivalry.

Once sharing snooker commentary with him. At the conclusion of play, Steve Davis's noisy entourage challenging us at the pool table. We didn't pay a single penny for our hotel that night because the 'master' proved to be a dangerous tactician, leaving me the easy task of potting. Eighteen frames in succession to the Welshmen.

A street corner in Cardiff, Carwyn in a hurry to return to Italy. 'Will you do me a favour?' 'Of course'. 'Hide this,' proffering a thick brown envelope. Spent an uncomfortable night roaming the city with enough money in my pocket to have bought a detached house in Radyr!

Seeing him for the last time in 1983. Just finished translating a script for him. He ignored my contribution. 'It'll be all right,' he said whilst embracing my son. He looked me straight in the eye. 'I'm going to Amsterdam for a rest'.

I head for home. We won't see Carwyn again.

John Evans

JAMES ALFORD

In this current era of Welsh athletics, we have come to expect such headlines as 'The Welsh Whirlwind' in the press, with the likes of Iwan Thomas, Colin Jackson and Jamie Baulch stealing the limelight and bringing honours to their country.

This was not the case in 1938, when that very headline appeared in an Australian newspaper during the Commonwealth Games staged at Sydney. It sent shockwaves throughout the athletic world and was really the first major breakthrough for the sport in Wales. Who was the hero of the hour?

None other than James William Llewelyn Alford, who later became the chief Welsh Athletics Coach. His achievement in winning the mile in 4 minutes 11.6 seconds was, at the time, simply phenomenal. In fact, the world had only ever

James Alford (second from left) in the back row.

seen the distance run faster on six previous occasions and never had such a time previously been achieved on Australian soil. He shattered the games record and his record was not to be broken until the 1949 Games, 11 years later.

Alford was expected to succeed in the half mile but a fellow competitor fell across his path and scuppered his chances of further glory. Following this disappointment, Alford was determined to prove himself over the mile.

The athletes got off to a flying start and the high tempo was sustained for the entire race, making it a thrilling encounter for all involved, the athletes and spectators alike. It was by no means a foregone conclusion; Alford, the eventual winner, was in seventh place at the end of the first quarter. Indeed, such was the intensity of the race that two runners failed to reach the finishing line.

Nevertheless, Alford's sheer determination reaped its rewards. The whole world not only wondered at his win but also appreciated his grace and discipline. He had that innate ability to run purposefully and beautifully, wasting no energy, and always showed tremendous physical and mental strength. He was the complete athlete.

Rahel Jones

IVOR ALLCHURCH

Wherever soccer is played, few players will have reached the standards achieved by Ivor Allchurch. The old Arsenal manager, Tom Whittaker, was unequivocal in ranking Allchurch as the 'player of the century'. An early recollection of him as a fellow pupil at Plasmarl Primary School in Swansea was of a shy 12 year old who usually found a quiet corner of the yard to practise soccer skills with a tennis ball, and I remember his mother coming to the school yard when he had failed to come home for tea and the remonstration invariably ended with the words 'all you think about is football'.

The shyness lasted throughout his life, and he often said that he preferred to express himself publicly with his feet – and he understood perfectly what was required of an inside-forward. It was the famous Spurs manager Bill Nicholson who once said after watching Allchurch that he had just witnessed 'the best inside-forward display I have ever seen'.

His ability to score fantastic goals with either foot has never been surpassed. I saw one of the very best when West Ham visited the Vetch Field in 1954. After scything through the midfield, his path to goal was covered by four defenders – John Bond, Malcolm Allison, Dave Sexton and Noel Cantwell no less. A deceptive body swerve gave him that extra space to crash a 25 yard shot into the roof of the net. The ultimate accolade came in the game against Hungary in the 1958 World Cup Finals when his goal, which helped Wales reach the quarter-final stage, was considered by most observers to be the goal of the competition.

Sir Matt Busby, the old Manchester United manager, said that the polish and class of this modest man puts him among the greatest players of all time.

Huw Phillips

W. J. BANCROFT

W. J. Bancroft was a daring, clever rugby player – one who played the game mentally as well as physically – with equally good running and kicking skills. He was a star full-back who played in that position 33 times for Wales, and captained his country 12 times; he was the first Welshman to win the triple crown twice. Bancroft was also one of the first players to engender something akin to patriotism, or national pride, in the magical game which Welshmen and -women claim as our national game, and he deserves to be remembered for that if nothing else.

In his poem 'Rygbi', the Swansea Valley poet Gwenallt suggested that, in the industrial towns of his youth, being Welsh didn't mean much; Alltwen was just a place where workers lived, eked out a meagre living to support a family. There was only one day when the workers of the coal mines and the steel works felt they were part of something greater, that they were part of a nation, and that was the day of the Wales-England International:

> Breuddwydiem drwy'r wythnos am ŵyl y Crysau Coch,
> A dyfod yn Sant Helen wyneb-yn-wyneb â'r Sais,
> A gwallgofi pan giciai Bancroft ei gôl Gymreig . . .

> [All week we'd dream of the red-shirt day,
> Facing the *Sais* on St Helen's battlefield,
> Euphoric as Bancroft kicked his Welsh goal . . .]

Rugby was a game for the Anglicized middle-classes in Wales, as in England, before Billy Bancroft's time. To most ordinary Welsh people in Victorian times, one's country and nation meant little other than the British Empire. Today we associate rugby with patriotism and its obvious external trappings; match day wouldn't be the same without the red white and green, the red dragons and the painted faces of Welshness. Billy Bancroft could never have foreseen this, but it was probably he who started it all.

Bethan Mair

GERALD BATTRICK

I suppose you could say that Gerald was a 'role model'. He was two years older than I was, and had already made his mark on the Junior Tennis Circuit in Wales. I had been brainwashed at an early age; it was rugby in the winter and tennis throughout the summer, with the facilities at the Bridgend Lawn Tennis Club providing the inspiration for a host of budding young sporting stars. Gerald was totally dedicated to his sport. His all-round shots and speed of thought, both mentally and physically, proved too much for the vast majority of his opponents.

To some extent I followed in his footsteps; from Bridgend Grammar School to Millfield and from Bridgend Lawn Tennis Club to the meticulously cut lawns of the All England Club at Wimbledon in SE19. Gerald was Junior Wimbledon Champion in 1964 and I followed suit in 1966 defeating David Lloyd (6-4, 6-4) in the final. These two results didn't meet with the approval of the Lawn Tennis

Association. They were totally obsessed with developing the game in England, and Wales wasn't on the map as far as they were concerned. The only individual who was totally supportive and determined to do his very utmost to develop the game throughout Britain was Dan Maskell; a true gentleman and very knowledgeable. He passed on his expertise to anyone who was prepared to listen and Gerald benefited greatly from his coaching.

Naturally, Gerald received very little publicity in his native land. If it's not rugby, football or cricket, the press and media aren't really interested. In fact, the tennis star from Mid Glamorgan never featured in the Top Ten Welsh Sporting Stars. The Welsh public were constantly craving for another John Charles or a Cliff Morgan, and tennis only courted attention during the Wimbledon fortnight when valley roads and public parks seemed jam-packed with budding young Lavers and Rosewalls.

Gerald Battrick represented Britain in the Davis Cup for many years, emulating Mike Davies from Swansea. He distinguished himself in major competitions, featured at Wimbledon, and proved a stubborn, skilful and all-round opponent. In later life he developed a tennis centre at his home in Waterton near Bridgend. His premature death was a sad loss to his family and to Welsh sport. He was a great competitor and a great man.

J. P. R. Williams

JAMIE BAULCH

From a sporting point of view athletics was my first love. Years before rugby tackled me head-on and knocked me sideways, it was track and field that occupied my teenage years. Hours spent training with Swansea Harriers certainly paid off. At the age of thirteen came my finest hour; West Glamorgan schools champion in the seventy-five metre hurdles.

You could say that I reached my peak too early, or even suffered from burnout, but let's face it, I was an average athlete, and for the next five years battled against that cruel truth. Olympic glory had been my dream, and if only my talents had matched my ambition!

Jamie Baulch on the other hand is one of those people whose natural ability is equal to their ambition. His type doesn't come along very often, and when they do, everybody knows about it. The talented kid in the running group always stands out like a formula one car racing a hatchback, a thoroughbred running with a bunch of donkeys. Baulch is class, and by now he is world class.

As a contemporary, I have followed Baulch's career in a subconscious fashion. Somehow he's always been around, from the dreadlocked youngster who used to train occasionally at the Morfa to the star he has now become in British Athletics. Baulch has a presence no one can ignore, especially his opponents.

Having sparkled as a junior at 200 metres, Baulch moved up to an event which some would argue is among the most difficult. To sprint a hundred metres is bad enough, but to do that four times on the trot is pretty gruelling. Moreover, Baulch isn't the tallest of athletes and therefore has to compensate with pace for what he loses in length of stride.

The decision to move up a distance has paid off and the Baulch record speaks for itself. Olympic silver in the four-by-four relay, World silver in the same event, a World finalist twice in the individual 400m, former World Indoor Champion. In addition, he's broken records galore along the way, most notably Todd Bennett's 12-year-old UK indoor record in 1997. Manchester 2002, beware.

Bethan Evans

PHIL BENNETT

We were checking our watches when the ball went loose on the Llanelli line. Immediately Phil Bennett picked it up, and in one movement he half turned to beat the first tackler, and before the rest could smother him he had lifted his kick into the grey October skies. Then, like a bowler drawing to the jack, he guided it into touch on the half-way line.

In that one moment of magic, Phil Bennett finished off the All Blacks. His quickness of mind had sniffed out the danger, his elusiveness had given him time and space, and his kick finished the job. He knew full well that rugby, to a large extent, is played in the mind; it is, as Carwyn James always stresses, a thinking game, and it was always Phil Bennett's hand that moved the pieces on the Stradey chessboard.

This was one moment in a big match; one moment of master-craftsmanship becoming artistry. Yet such glimpses of brilliance were regularly repeated week in, week out over the season. Looking back through my scarlet-tinted spectacles I cannot recall any of his punts missing the mark, more than I can remember J. P. R. dropping a high ball.

There were other matches for Wales, the Barbarians and the Lions, where he consistently thrilled the crowds on the world's biggest stages. But the beauty of his little cameo is that it took place in Llanelli's colours at Stradey Park in front of his own people. There, in Scarletland, like Albert Jenkins before him, he reigned supreme. He was very much a product of the town's passion, of its warm socialism. Llanelli created him. Yet, like twenty thousand others, I would like to think that it was the other way around and that, in one moment of brilliance, it was Phil Bennett that created Llanelli.

Idris Reynolds

JOHN C. BEVAN

Wings to excite and delight. Runners of percussive power or the darting dance of the butterfly. Cardiff have enjoyed them all; names to recall with pride, admiration and even wonder. We tend to compare wings with the unmatchable Gerald Davies, which is horribly unfair. There always will be a wide variation of styles, and they all play their part in enriching the game, as they have done so imaginatively for Cardiff and the Arms Park cognoscenti. Since full-time rugby resumed after Hitler's arrogant interference with events, Cardiff continued to benefit from their production line of renowned runners. There was, perhaps, the most popular of uncapped wings, P. L. 'Lyn' Jones, a 'galloping gunner' who brought his scoring power to bear with 120 club tries. His was raw energy and a 'bullet proof' rib cage as he bumped off many determined tacklers.

For style, you needed to look elsewhere. Such as Haydn Morris, the smooth, gliding sudden-death specialist; the dapper Steve Hughes (73 tries), Les Williams, Keri Jones and the lightning thrust of the jet-like Olympic hurdler Nigel Walker. Maurice Richards was another of immense talent and huge scoring potential (97 club tries). Derek Murphy (77 tries), Howard Nicholls (68 tries), Dr Gwyn Rowlands (66 tries), Terry Cook, Russell Burn, D. H. Jones, Rev. Howard Loveluck, Steve McGann, Frank Wilson and C. L. 'Cowboy' Davies. They were dashers, sprinters, schemers; some with that little bit of magic in their boots; others with the spirit of the Charge of the Light Brigade.

Then there was John C. Bevan, the Tylorstown Terror, man of menace whenever he attacked the line. To unleash him was to let loose a tornado; a terrifying vision to some whose unenviable task was to stop a human missile zooming for the corner-flag. Battering-ram shoulders, explosive hand-off, hips of steel, he wore the red jersey of Wales ten times in what was an all too brief time in the RU game before Warrington snapped him up to make him yet another Welsh legend under the RL spotlight with more than 200 tries. J. C. scored a debut try against England and was top try-scorer for the 1971 Lions with 18 tries. His 17 in New Zealand (after two matches in Australia) equalled the record in that country by Ireland's Tony O'Reilly in 1959. If any Welsh wing deserves to be compared with the giant All Blacks' super-hero Jonah Lomu it has to be crash-bash Bevan. Move that brick wall quickly – before he hits it down.

John Billot

BILLY BOSTON

Billy Boston left Tiger Bay and the union code for Wigan and rugby league in 1953. He had never represented Wales before his move to the north of England and the links with the land of his birth have become ever more tenuous. A big, powerful man, blessed with a dazzling array of skills, Boston went on to set and shatter numerous Wigan club records.

During his career Boston scored 572 tries, a figure second only in the record books to the Australian winger Brian Bevan, and a number yet to be surpassed by any other British player. He scored 478 tries for Wigan, smashing the previous club record of Johnny Ring's by more than a hundred. He held the league's try-scoring record with sixty tries in the 1956-57 season and scored more than fifty in 1958-59 and 1961-62.

Billy also won representative honours for Wales and Great Britain, touring down under in 1954 and 1962. In thirty-four internationals, thirty-one of which were tests, Boston scored thirty tries, including ten against Australia, a record which still stands today.

But facts and figures, although impressive, cannot re-create or conjure the image of Boston in full flow. A right winger, Boston could play anywhere across the back-line with equal ease and guile. When he initially signed for Wigan as a nineteen year old, he had the speed and swerve of Martin Offiah, the side step of a Gerald Davies, a big heart and the footballing brain of an instinctive creator. Ten years later, as a legendary player, he still maintained his pace but had added a thuddering hand-off and an immense muscular bulk to the frame of the original signing from Tiger Bay. The physical transformation of Scott Gibbs during his time at League seems a striking parallel.

During the 1950s and 1960s, Wigan was an industrial town suffering economic and social hangovers dating from the Second World War and earlier. Thus the pleasures of viewing Boston's genius on a gloomy Saturday afternoon became a delight. He was a bright beacon in the smog of the industrial North. In a peculiar way, Wigan could have replicated Tiger Bay in the mind of Billy Boston. Although lacking the ethnic communities and different cultures of Cardiff's docklands, the tight-knit community, the love of rugby and the welcome he received on the playing fields of Wigan presented Boston with an equality of opportunity that he felt he might never have gained in the world of union in Wales (it was on a tour to South Africa that Boston suffered his only racial prejudice during his connection with league). League was a more cosmopolitan game, and Wigan was one of the most racially varied sides.

The warmth of the streets of Tiger Bay, where Billy had been friendly with Shirley Bassey and Joe Erskine, echoed in his acceptance in the pubs and clubs of Wigan as Billy Boston, rugby league virtuoso.

Tomos Williams

DAVID BROOME

December back in the seventies; and whilst everyone in Glanaman, the Amman Valley and the rest of the world looked forward with anticipation to Christmas, I counted the days to a very special sporting occasion – the Horse of the Year Show at Olympia in London.

Football, rugby, netball, music, films and cartoons proved to be the main focus of attention as far as my fellow pupils at the local primary school were concerned. To be honest, horses and especially show-jumping had interested me from an early age, just after I jilted Father Christmas. For a week prior to the festive celebrations, the crème de la crème of the show-jumping fraternity came together at Olympia and competed in one of the most prestigious of events. I seem to recall that the action continued on BBC television until way after my bedtime but any attempts to dislodge me from my debenture in front of our Bush 24-inch set met with a stern disapproval.

My hero was David Broome from the Chepstow area, a Welshman from rural Monmouthshire. The talented, disciplined and outstanding horseman challenged the world's premier showjumpers for a period of more than twenty years. He would have needed a terrace of stables to keep all the cups and trophies

accumulated during his competitive period. One of the main competitions was the Grand Prix; the riders had to master a series of difficult fences, culminating in a furious final gallop around the arena against the clock. However, my favourite event was the Puissance; the first few fences were fairly straightforward but the final fence resembled a prison wall. The height of this fence was changed as each rider succeeded; bricks were added by the marshals, causing considerable consternation to horse and rider (and viewers at home!).

David Broome was at home in this environment. His preparations were always meticulous, and his horses were always at ease in the frenzied atmosphere that prevailed at these shows. Whilst my friends at school hero-worshipped Sebastian Coe, Tessa Sanderson, Terry Holmes and Ian Rush, I wanted to follow in David Broome's footsteps and collect the silver cups and winners' ribbons from the ever-present royalty.

To some extent my dream was realised. Not that I excelled in the field of show-jumping, but I frequently came across my boyhood idol at local shows, especially the Gower Show where he often accompanied his son who is an enthusiastic rider. He always passes on some valuable tips to other competitors – a sign of a great man. I often witnessed his natural ability in the saddle – the gentle hands, that innate ability to bring out the best in his mounts, the confidence that stemmed from his upbringing and the genius that enabled him to time his jumps to perfection. These were some of the skills which thrilled the spectators at Olympia and which hypnotised a young child watching enthusiastically from the comfort of 19, Tircoed Road, Glanaman.

The travelling and the competitions came to an end, but the cameos are still etched in celluloid in my mind. Definitely not pictures of the noisy Yorkshireman Harvey Smith, certainly not reels of film relating to the adventurous Irishman, Eddie Macken. My recollections revolve around the Welshman on his white horse. He was a true master in our home during that week prior to the Christmas celebrations.

Huw Rees

JOE CALZAGHE

Joe Calzaghe entered the professional ranks as a multiple ABA titleholder and was guided initially by Mickey Duff and Terry Lawless, two of boxing's most influential characters. He made his professional debut in October 1993, stopping Paul Hanlon in the first round. A series of quick wins followed, and it was not until February 1995 that he went the distance for the first time, beating Bobbie Joe Edwards over eight rounds.

Joe won the British Supermiddleweight title, stopping Stephen Wilson in eight rounds at that most historic and atmospheric of venues, the Royal Albert Hall. He now felt he deserved a shot at the world crown, and in frustration left Duff and Lawless for the Frank Warren camp.

Following the retirement of Steve Collins, he was matched with Chris Eubank for the world crown in October 1997. He floored Eubank in the first round and again in the tenth but had to settle for a well-deserved points victory.

15

Life was sweet as world champion, but he was soon plagued by a series of injuries and these resulted in less than convincing defences against Robin Reid, Rick Thornberry and David Starie, but Joe was back to his very best in stopping Omar Sheika in five rounds at Wembley in August 2000. The power displayed earlier in his career had returned, as had the confidence and momentum in his work, and he ended the year with a performance of the highest quality in stopping Richie Woodhall in ten rounds at Sheffield. It was unfortunate that the quality of this display was overshadowed on the night by the injuries sustained by Paul Ingle.

Joe and father Enzo, his long-time trainer, dream of making a big impression in America and having now overwhelmed Mario Veit, Wales's most successful world champion deserves the opportunity of testing himself in the toughest of schools.

Wynford Jones

JOHN CHARLES

To my eternal regret, I never saw John Charles play. It was nothing personal – I just wasn't old enough. As I was starting to walk and talk in the 1950s, the Gentle Giant was striding across the world stage, making friends and influencing people. John Charles was a megastar long before the word was invented, but sadly, by the time I became interested in the beautiful game, the career of one of its greatest exponents was all but over.

It wasn't until I began writing Cardiff City's centenary celebration, in 1999, that I became aware of his awesome ability. During the making of a BBC Wales television documentary to accompany the book, I discovered some grainy footage of the great man in action. I marvelled as he powered in a far-post header from a right-wing cross in the black and white stripes of Juventus. The defenders weren't fouled; they simply failed to match his magnificent athleticism as the ball flashed into the net from his formidable forehead. 'Il gigante buono' may have summed up the temperament of this 6' 2" talisman yet his finishing was anything but gentle.

John Charles was almost as prodigious with Wales for whom he scored 15 goals in 38 internationals. He made an inauspicious debut against Northern Ireland at Wrexham in 1950 in a game so dull that one woman fell asleep in the Racecourse stand. Eight years later, had he been fit, Wales might not have lost to Pele's first goal for Brazil in the World Cup quarter-finals.

After being switched from centre-half to centre-forward at Leeds, this remarkable Swansea Jack really made his mark in Italy. Where John Charles led, Law, Greaves, Hitchens and, much later, Rush followed, but none could match the multi-talented trail-blazer from Cwmbwrla. In the most defensive league in the world, he netted 28 goals in his first season with Juventus. During his five years with the club, he scored 93 times in 155 appearances as they won the Italian League three times and the Cup twice.

An ill-fated move to Leeds and then to Roma was followed by a return to the green, green grass of home – not back to Swansea but to Cardiff City. Hereford United – before their giant-killing exploits of the early Seventies – and Merthyr were his last two ports of call. Unfortunately, retirement has been anything but gentle and John has recently been fighting a battle against cancer.

They say John Charles was the most accomplished footballer of his generation. Indeed, many claim he was the finest ever produced by Wales. I may have not seen him play

in the flesh but I am more than happy to rely on that archive footage – and the opinions of older and wiser judges who swear that John Charles was indeed a giant, if not a colossus, among men.

Grahame Lloyd

ROBERT CROFT

Whether it's third bong on the *News* headlines, a song on the balcony or a long bowl in the middle, Robert Croft is never from the spotlight. Like every great Welsh sportsman down the ages, 'Crofty' oozes the passion, hwyl and will to succeed.

With twenty-one Tests and fifty one-day internationals under his belt so far, he is by far the most experienced Welshman to play for England. A dragon in the lion's den! He sees playing for Glamorgan like turning out for Wales, while England is the equivalent of representing the British Lions.

But although he has played for England much more than his Glamorgan contemporaries, such as Matthew Maynard, Hugh Morris and Steve Watkin, he has been dealt plenty of disappointments since making his test debut in 1996 against Pakistan. Just when he looked like getting a run in the England side he was dropped or overlooked. When he recorded figures of 5-95 against New Zealand at Christchurch in the 1996-97 series, a long international career had seemed assured.

But even though Croft can probably feel he has been treated shabbily, it hasn't affected the off-spinner's burning passion to succeed. He wears a daffodil close to his heart and red, green and white blood runs through his veins. His most memorable season to date was 1997 when he was at the forefront of Glamorgan's championship winning efforts and when he made the ITN *News at Ten* on a steamy August day at Chelmsford.

After sealing the championship against Somerset, Croft led a jubilant crowd in a rendition of 'Alhouette' from the Taunton balcony. Only a month earlier, Croft had got himself in trouble with the cricket authorities when he was involved in a pushing incident with his great friend Mark Ilott in that now infamous NatWest trophy semi-final against Essex. The flashpoint occurred because Croft was just so desperate for Glamorgan to win a Lord's final – something you just feel is fated for a player of Crofty's passion before the end of his career.

Richard Thomas

BRIAN CURVIS

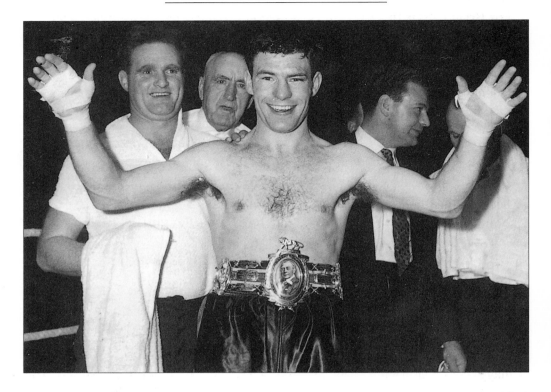

The great Emile Griffith came to London to put his treasured world title on the line in September 1964, which was probably a year or so too late for the well-being and ambition of his brave Welsh challenger.

Brian Curvis put up a show all right. We always knew he would. The British champion, who was as Swansea as Mumbles Pier, had never failed to give of his best. Not for nothing was the man who fitted the often abused description of a 'professional's professional' respected by all through the toughest sporting pusuit known by man.

But when the accomplished Griffith at last succumbed to mounting pressure to give the Welshman his deserved tilt at the world welterweight crown, many of us feared that, although he was still only 27, Curvis's best days might just be behind him.

And so it proved. Wembley on that night of high emotion was no place for the squeamish, as two giants of their calling went about their brutal trade in the only way they knew how. Unfortunately, although a stirring contest went the scheduled 15 rounds, there were few prepared to disagree that the better man had won. Griffith, the teak-tough Virgin Islander who had reigned as the best around on and off between 1961 and 1966, kept the title in his bag for the return home to the States.

For Brian Curvis there was to be no second chance. The destiny predicted for him since he was big enough to lace on a glove in a family where boxing was as much a way of life as the local docks which provided the employment to fuel ambition of glory in the ring had been cruelly denied him.

He hung around for a couple more years, confident in the knowledge that there was no one remotely good enough on the domestic scene to remove him from his reign as undefeated British and Commonwealth champion between 1960 and 1966. A record of just four defeats in 41 contests and ownership of two Lonsdale Belts was a comfort to take into retirement.

But it could have been so much better had the reluctant Griffith been tempted to accept a justified challenge a little earlier, before an annoying run of injury and minor set-backs had blunted much of the Welshman's feared cutting edge.

Norman Lewis

GERALD DAVIES

It may have taken Tina Turner until the late 80s to come out with 'Simply The Best' – a song which has since been adopted as an anthem in all kinds of sporting fields – but Gerald Davies could have laid claim to the title a decade earlier as far as rugby wingers were concerned.

Born in the village of Llansaint and educated at Queen Elizabeth Grammar School, Carmarthen, Loughborough College and Cambridge University, Gerald's international career extended from 1966 to 1978. He won 46 Welsh caps – the first 11 coming at centre – and scored 20 tries. He also went on two Lions tours, to South Africa in 1968 and New Zealand in 1971, and his try-scoring exploits in the latter, in particular, assured him legendary status in the Southern as well as the Northern Hemisphere

But these are merely the bald facts of an illustrious career which provided countless highlights and memories for rugby followers all over the world. Gerald's trademarks were his blistering pace, superbly balanced running, a lovely swerve and a massive side-step that has yet to be replicated. His free spirit and adventurous style, largely nurtured in his days with a highly successful London Welsh team, were typified in the way that he started the counter attack almost from his own try-line, which resulted in Phil Bennett's try at Murrayfield in 1977, one of the all time great tries in the Five Nations Championship.

21

Six years previously, at the same ground, everyone remembers John Taylor's dramatic touch-line conversion to give Wales a late 19-18 win, but it was Gerald Davies's clinical finishing, when there was a great deal of work to do, that made such a win possible. And perhaps nowhere was Gerald better able to demonstrate his deadly finishing skills than during his second spell at Cardiff. The venue was Pontypool Park in the 3rd round of the 1978 Schweppes Cup. With the Pooler pack in their hey-day, they totally dominated up front, securing more than 90% possession. Cardiff could string together no more than half a dozen attacks throughout, but despite the heavy pitch, the intimidating atmosphere and the importance of the occasion, Gerald Davies scored four memorable tries from those six attacks. Cardiff, incredibly, won 16-11.

In his playing days, and as a reporter since then, Gerald Davies has never lost his enthusiasm and the sense of wonder that rugby can bring. Nor has he ever lost his humility or gentlemanly qualities. A deep thinker on rugby and life in general . . . always a joy to watch and always a pleasure to be in his company, Gerald Davies is indeed 'Simply the Best'.

Gareth Charles

HYWEL DAVIES

Without doubt, Hywel Davies, the affable 'Cardi', is one of Wales's most successful jockeys of all time. His success on 'Last Suspect' in the 1985 Grand National brought him instant stardom, but one mustn't forget his other notable successes in a glittering career, namely 'Gophar' in the Hennessey Gold Cup, 'Topsham Bay' in the Whitbread, as well as two outstanding rides in the Queen Mother Champion Chase at the Cheltenham Festival on board 'Barnbrook Again' and 'Katabatic.'

Hywel was born in 1956, the youngest of the three sons of Meurig and 'Maj' Davies, and as Dad was a blacksmith, the interest in horses was there from an early age. Yet it was the Cuff family, the owners of 'Plas Llangoedmor' a mile or so outside Cardigan, who polished up the riding and jumping skills of the young Davies, as he collected prizes galore at the Royal Welsh, Stoneleigh and even Hickstead.

He left Cardigan Grammar School, where a contemporary of his was Jonathan Jones, the World Powerboat Champion, at the age of 16, and spent a couple of years 'cutting his teeth' on the Point to Point circuit. Yet, thanks largely to the intuition of his elder brother, Geraint, he was given his chance at the age of 19 at the famous Findon Stables of Josh Gifford (who would win the National himself with 'Aldaniti'). Three seasons later, he was appointed stable jockey to Roddy Armytage, riding 81 winners over two seasons, before landing the plum job of stable jockey to the late Captain Tim Forster, trainer of three Grand National winners.

Hywel retired from riding in 1994, largely because of weight problems, but his career has blossomed, with his outgoing, bubbly personality no doubt playing a

part in his media work as a racing and trotting pundit in his beloved Wales, whilst of late he has successfully managed the 'Winning Line', who own several top racehorses. Cardigan and Wales can justifiably be proud of the achievements of one of the nation's greatest ever riders.

Alun Tudur Jenkins

JONATHAN DAVIES

Every now and again a god is born in the Welsh valleys. He bears a simple name of the people, like Barry John, or Phil Bennett, or Gareth Edwards; and for twenty years or so he grows up like any normal human being. But the word spreads that he can perform magic and feats of superhuman skill with an oval ball, and the people come to see, and they recognise that he is the saviour for whom they have been waiting.

There has been a dearth of such gods of late, but a young man has now been found and the process of deification has begun. Like so many precious Welsh gods, Jonathan Davies plays at fly-half. He does so in a way which has provoked some witnesses, not usually known for their softness of brain, to claim that he is not merely one of the chosen few, but supreme among them.

The last few years have been the worst in many decades for Welsh rugby. The national side has been mediocre and, worse, boring to watch; the club scene has been dominated by accusations of excessive on-the-field violence, some exaggerated but much of it depressingly true.

Enter Jonathan Davies, who dazzles without thuggery, who plays the game almost whimsically, obeying no plan other than his instinct, whose speed of foot and mind have not been seen in the valleys for many a long year. The comparisons are with George Best, Alex Higgins and Ian Botham, sportsmen who have the capacity to play their game with a brilliance and originality that defies rational analysis and engenders thoughts of witchcraft. It is no accident that these are among Davies's heroes; happily, he has not yet learnt their flaws of character.

There is a difference between excellence and genius which is hard to define, but impossible to miss when confronted with it. 'The first time I saw him, even before he touched the ball, I knew that he was something special. It was like seeing Gary Sobers coming in to bat and taking guard. You don't often experience that feeling in your life,' says Cliff Morgan, himself a fly-half god of Wales.

He quotes the lines of Wilfred Owen : 'Courage was mine, and I had mystery/ Wisdom was mine, and I had mastery.' I believe that Davies has mastery and mystery. He has everything and, most important, he has confidence and an arrogance about his own ability.'

The word arrogance is used by everyone who talks about Davies. It is meant admiringly, not critically, to describe a player so far above the ordinary that an element of disdainful superiority is inevitable. 'He knows he has these skills, and wants to demonstrate them,' explains Gerald Davies, magical Welsh winger of the 1970s and Jonathan Davies's rugby hero. 'He shows off, but he takes risks. He does outrageous things which come off. He's brought sparkle and adventure back to the Welsh game.'

Phil Bennett, another member of rugby's Olympus, marvels at his incredible speed and acceleration. He describes with awe the contemptuous ease with which Davies swerves, sidesteps, and glides past defenders. 'He's absolutely brilliant. When he's playing for Neath, even on a cold and rainy Tuesday evening, you think twice about staying at home.'

The ultimate compliment for a Welsh fly-half is to be compared to King Barry John, peerlessly elegant god of the late sixties and early seventies. Cliff Morgan does not shirk from putting Davies on the same pedestal. Brian Thomas, team manager of Davies's club Neath, goes further, 'He's got a few qualities that John never had. For one thing, he's got an aggressive defence. He tackles, and tackles hard. He's got everything. He can run, he can kick, he can handle, he can pass and he can tackle. He's got it all, and he's got it to a greater degree and at a younger age than anyone I've seen in my life. And he's getting better all the time.'

Marcel Berlins
Times Newspapers Ltd 1987

LYNN DAVIES

I shall never forget, I don't think, that bleak Sunday evening in Japan. Not that I was there, but such is the indelible image that has seared itself into my memory, that I have begun to think over time that I was there. The black and white pictures which migrated across the continents to reach our homes made the Meiji stadium look bleaker than it in fact was. Lynn Davies from Nantymoel cut a lonely figure in the windswept and rain-soaked Tokyo night; the local boy so far from home, as we all thought of him, and playing to win the long jump against overwhelming odds. It was the stuff of dreams and adventure. This was the Olympics, sport's greatest theatre, when a Welshman stood on the edge of immortality.

We are accustomed in Wales to seek our heroes on the playing fields, more particularly in both the football codes of soccer and rugby union. Perhaps this is partly because we can translate the strong sense of belonging and togetherness which we have traditionally found in our communities into the team spirit which inspires these games. Much like silver bands and choirs, we find that they are shared experiences. No doubt we also enjoy the thrills and spills that rugby and soccer excitingly provide.

In 1964, Wales found for itself a different kind of hero, one who ran on a track, not grass, and who wore a delicate pair of spikes on his feet, not a ponderous pair of football boots. Lynn Davies stood as a solitary figure who chose a different route to the status of a legend in Wales and beyond. He pursued his talent on the athletics track, isolated and single-minded.

Others had chosen this path and had themselves made their genuine and unforgettable mark. No one, however, had won an Olympic gold medal on the athletics track. The only other famous gold medal, so the wits would have it, could be said to have been won on four not two legs. (The great Harry Llewellyn had won his on a horse, Foxhunter).

Against the outstanding favourites to win – Ralph Boston of the USA and Igor Terovanesyan of the USSR – Lynn was meant to dent their reputations, not overcome them. The newspapers show the famous leap with a head-on picture, arms swirling in the air, while the moving image on our flickering television screens showed how, after accomplishing his successful jump, he turns and takes a little skip of knowing delight. The gold medal was his.

It was a remarkable achievement. As a new millennium commences, he remains Wales' single athletics gold. In Tokyo's gloom Lynn Davies left the vivid air signed with his honour.

Gerald Davies

MERVYN DAVIES

Thomas Mervyn Davies can easily lay claim to membership of a special band of rugby performers from the hundreds who have donned the famous red shirt of Wales. His days with the three feathers proudly perched on his left breast coincided with the golden era of the '70s and an universal acknowledgement of their magical deeds.

Put simply, the familiar beanpole figure with the trademark headband interrupting his long sideburned bushy hairstyle was known as just Merve, or, to give him his full name, Merve the Swerve. The Christian-name status conferred on Davies and his other illustrious contemporaries was merely confirmation of a rugby mad nation's gratitude and affection for their part in delivering a feel-good factor to Wales.

He took his place in the Welsh line-up for the first time at Murrayfield in 1969; a tall, rangy number 8 who had impressed in the London Welsh team, playing rugby as it should be played. The attacking-minded ethos of the Old Deer Park outfit gave Davies the perfect platform to display skills that made him

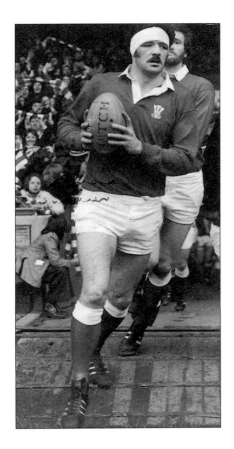

the consummate player of his time in the position.

Restrictions on kicking the ball straight out had been brought in, freeing the game in the process, and Davies was one who took full advantage to show off his footballing abilities. A modern ball-winning exponent, he was also able to bring the potent backs alongside him into devastating play for club, country and the British Lions on winning, ground-breaking tours of New Zealand and South Africa.

He came back to Wales and his native Swansea to continue the performance which was rudely and nearly fatally interrupted by a brain haemorrhage in the field of play against Pontypool in 1976. The career of Wales's Grand Slam captain of a few weeks earlier was over, but his reputation as one of Wales's finest remains to this day.

Chris Peregrine

MICHAEL DAVIES

One of my earliest childhood memories is focused on my fascination for catching newts as I watched them darting to and fro in a pond in a field located close to my home in Swansea. This same field bore traces of a number of tennis courts that had existed there many years earlier. During my teenage years I remember having heard a story about someone who had also practised and played on this same field. His name was Michael Davies.

Michael's meteoric rise to fame, ultimately becoming one of the leading tennis players of his day during the 1950s, is remarkable, bearing in mind that no other Welshman had ever before, or since, achieved such fame. His interest in the game was sparked at an early age when he borrowed his aunt's tennis racquet. At first it was a case of hitting tennis balls against the wall of his house, but he soon graduated to the aforementioned tennis courts, at nearby Rosehill.

His absolute dedication and enthusiastic approach to the game were such that by the age of ten his exceptional abilities prompted him to embark on a career as a professional; a decision which met with his parents' ready approval and support. Michael Davies's success during this period included winning the Welsh Under 16's championship three years in succession. In due course, this outstanding talent came under the scrutiny of the British Lawn Tennis Association, who selected him for individual coaching under the guidance of Dan Maskell and Fred Paulson.

There followed a visit to Australia sponsored by a Cardiff businessman, where Michael Davies received further coaching from the world's leading coach, Harry Hoperean. This paid dividends and enabled Michael to participate in tournaments far and wide. In the early stages, this proved difficult on account of financial restraints. However, sound performances allowed him to achieve a measure of financial independence. On his return to the United Kingdom, he continued to succeed in major tournaments. He reached his peak in 1957, when he was selected to represent Great Britain in the Davies Cup in France. Davies achieved a remarkable victory in one of the Singles matches over Robert Haillet in front of a crowd of 12,000 patriotic Frenchmen.

His crowning glory came during 1960 when, partnered by R. K. (Bob) Wilson, he reached the final of the Men's Doubles event at Wimbledon, only to be narrowly defeated by Osuna and Ralston. To this day people still talk about his incredible fitness and athleticism, his strong and fast serve, devestating forearm drives and delicate forehand and backhand lobs. Michael Davies truly deserves to be recorded in the annals of Welsh sporting history.

Carolyn Walters

TERRY DAVIES

Terry Davies was a full-back in the traditional, classical, pre-1968 mould – the last line of defence. He possessed an instinctive positioning sense, which allowed him to deal with a variety of kicks – high up and unders, diagonal kicks, and cross-kicks; very safe hands and a fielding technique, which rarely saw him drop the ball; and a physique strong and solid enough to withstand would-be tacklers (remember Mannetjies Roux, South Africa?), and then put the ball away safely to touch. This sense of positioning also put him in the right place at the right time to make try-saving tackles. Many a time I heard Terry say that far too many full-backs were not blamed for dropping the ball, or for missing a tackle, because they were not in position to accomplish the tasks in the first place. He himself relished the challenges posed by the opposition, meeting them all with a supreme self-confidence.

Terry had all the above skills in abundance. However, the skill that, for me, set him apart, was his phenomenal kicking – both place-kicking (toe-style) and punting. During my close association with him at Llanelli, first as his understudy, and then as his successor, I spent a lot of time on training night practising kicking with him. I will never forget one occasion, when he asked me to stand at the point where the touch and half-way lines meet, and then punted the ball from under the posts on the Pwll end of Stradey Park, directly over my head and into touch; a tremendous demonstration of length and accuracy. It was touch kicking of a kind that he repeated time and again in games, and, as I mention above, set him apart from most full backs playing in world rugby at the time.

The best way to illustrate his place-kicking prowess is to refer to the Welsh victory over Ireland at the Cardiff Arms Park in 1957, when Terry kicked two penalties out of a morass of mud, to win the game for Wales, 6 points to 3. It was amazing, considering the condition under foot, that the heavy ball even got off the ground, let alone travelled the 35-40 yards over the bar. Again, it was a remarkable demonstration of the strength of his kicking, the purity of his technique, and the total belief he had in his own ability.

Finally, there is one aspect of his game which is not often appreciated, and that was his ability to initiate counter-attacks out of defence. This leads me to the belief, that, were he playing now, in the post-1968 era, then his athleticism, pace, and feel for the game would have made him equally as successful as he was in the traditional role of last line of defence. For me, he was the complete full-back.

John Elgar Williams

VALERIE DAVIES

An initial assessment of the Games held at Los Angeles in 1932 would indicate a disappointing chapter in the history of the Olympic Movement. Several countries were not represented due to the recession incurred by the Wall Streeet Crash of 1929. However, the Los Angeles Olympic Games were an undisputed success as far as Valerie Davies was in question, with the twenty-one year old swimmer from Cardiff winning two bronze medals; one in the 100 metre backstroke race and another as a member of the British female relay team.

Valerie Davies was the daughter of a Cardiff shipping merchant, and she was a natural swimmer. She could swim by the age of five, following three lessons in a paddling pool in Barry. However, this budding athlete was nine before her talent was recognised. Whilst competing in races across Roath Lake she was spotted by a trainer who advised her parents to seek professional training for their daughter so that her talent could be properly developed. Since there was no indoor pool in Cardiff at that time, Valerie had to travel to London in order to train during the winter months. The young girl soon became one of the most talented swimmers in Britain.

At fifteen, Valerie, having won fourteen championships in Wales, was chosen to take part in the European Games in Bologna in 1927. She was the youngest member of the swimming team. Unexpectedly, the female relay team won the Gold Medal and the press paid much attention to the pretty, dark-haired girl from Cardiff. In 1930 it was Valerie Davies who carried the Red Dragon flag in the opening ceremony of the Empire Games which were held for the first time in Hamilton, Canada. Once again she was successful, winning four medals in the competition.

By 1932, many were of the opinion that Valerie stood a good chance of a medal in one of the individual categories in Los Angeles. The Olympic team sailed to New York before embarking upon a four-day train journey across the United States. Having arrived in Los Angeles, the girls stayed in a hotel for three weeks, and during this time there was no opportunity to practise prior to the competitions. The lack of facilities did not impair Valerie Davies's performance; she was the only British swimmer to reach a final:

> *All I did was swim . . . and swim . . . and swim again. When I touched the wall I was unaware of my success until an official notified me that I was in third place and had won a bronze medal. It was difficult to believe it; I had never expected such success.* (Interview in *The Western Mail*, 1996).

The Empire Games in London in 1934 was her last international competition, and Valerie was the Welsh team captain. At twenty-three years of age, Valerie Davies had decided to retire.

Nêst Llywelyn Lewis

JOHN DISLEY

The '50s provided Wales with by far the most significant sporting festival ever staged in the country. The sixth British Empire and Commonwealth Games in 1958 enabled the Welsh sporting public to witness firsthand some of the greatest sportsmen and sportswomen in the world at Cardiff Arms Park.

During the decade, Wales's outstanding athlete was undoubtedly John Disley. Born in Corris on November 20th 1928, he became Britain's first world-class steeplechaser for 15 years when he set four British records at two miles and five at 3000 metres. He smashed through the 9-minute barrier at the 1952 Olympics in Helsinki when he improved from 9.11.80 to 8.51.94 for the bronze medal. He only missed the silver medal by 2/100ths of a second.

John Disley (No. 1) out in front with 400 metres remaining.

His Olympic medal was the first ever to be won by a Welshman in an individual track event. Only Colin Jackson has achieved this feat since. He was world ranked in the steeplechase – 3rd in 1952, 2nd in 1955, 6th in 1956 and 9th in 1957. Disley made the 1956 Olympic team for Melbourne and despite running 8m 44.6 seconds, he could only finish sixth in a race surprisingly won by his friend Chris Brasher in 8m 41.2 seconds.

It was, however, his misfortune and greatest regret that the steeplechase was not included in the Commonwealth Games programme between 1934 and 1962. In 1958 he was still good enough to be ranked second in the Commonwealth but was denied the opportunity of representing his country on home soil at Cardiff. In front of fanatical Welsh fans, he would surely have won a gold medal!

The European Championships in 1950 (Brussels) and 1954 (Berne) were not happy occasions, as he could only finish thirteenth (no time recorded) and tenth (9m 07.6 seconds) respectively. During his career he ran for London Athletic Club and was a schoolmaster, and despite missing out in 1958 on wearing the three feathers, he gained 19 British vests between 1950 and 1957.

Educated at Oswestry High School in Shropshire, he had never seen an athletic track until he came to Loughborough College as a student in 1946. Before that, his running had been confined to annual cross-country runs and school sports.

He took the Welsh mile title three times (1949, 1951 and 1958) and the British AAA steeplechase title also on three occasions (1952, 1955 and 1957). He was a member of the International Orienteering Federation (1972-78) and was a leading pioneer of the sport in Britain. He was awarded the CBE in 1979 for his work in outdoor education, and was vice-chairman of the Sports Council (1974-82). He is also director of the London Marathon.

Mike Walters

DAI DOWER

The chance to fight for the World Featherweight crown came unexpectedly for the Abercynon wizard in 1955. Unluckily for him, he was two stone overweight, and had already lost the European title to Young Martin of Spain in a bitter contest.

With three weeks to go before the trip to Argentina to face the hammer-blows of Pascual Perez, he *had* to lose weight. And what happened? By the time Dower got to Buenos Aires, he was so weak that he had no hope of withstanding the powerful fists of Perez, and lost the bout in the first round! Thousands of disappointed radio listeners back in Wales couldn't believe their ears.

Nevertheless, Dower became a popular hero of the Valleys by securing the British and European championship after representing Britain at the Olympic Games in Helsinki in 1952. Boxing was in his blood, and after showing early promise, the light-as-a-feather youngster had to move to Bournemouth where an uncle worked as a chef in a hotel, and was better-placed to feed the tiny fighter.

Dower was a very quick boxer, with a gift for dodging his opponents with both speedy feet and swift thinking. It was a pleasure to watch him in the ring; his dancing feet even mesmerized his opponent. In those days of sustained competition, with fighters climbing into the ring far more frequently than today, being crowned champion was a true feat.

In contrast to many who suffered the physical results of this harsh sport, Dower retired early and went on to become a PE teacher, and then the administrator of Bournemouth University's Sports Centre. By now he has retired, but he still plays cricket! He isn't overly keen on modern boxing; 'Not enough talent,' he says, 'and too much of a circus. Naseem is obviously gifted, for example, but I can't stand all the acting and the hype which is such a part of the sport nowadays.'

Martyn Williams

JIM DRISCOLL

If Jim Driscoll had been American, to try and do him justice in 300 words might be seen as something of a joke. It certainly seems a shame that, whereas the memories of so many 'heroes' who could have had class, and could have been contenders, are kept alive on film and in books and at award ceremonies, while sports-faculty buildings bear their names, a man who actually had class, and who was never less than a contender in every one of his seventy-odd fights, is, for the most part, forgotten.

And it's ironic, then, or more probably inevitable, that he should have had to travel to the country where you ain't nobody unless you're 'Iron Mike' or 'Smokin Joe' or even 'The Greatest', to become 'Peerless Jim', and to 'make his name'. If Jim Driscoll had been American, the biographies and film scripts as good as write themselves: all you have to do is substitute Hell's Kitchen for Bute Street, the Bronx for the Old Plantation, clear your old bowls trophies out of the cabinet, put your feet up and wait for the Golden Globes . . .

Driscoll, a boxer out of the same social 'necessity' as Muhammed Ali, grew up fighting in fairground booths, taking on all comers, even giants, challenging anybody to hit him in the face if they could, while he stood on a handkerchief, bobbing and weaving, with his hands tied behind his back. And then, in 1909, he beat Abe Attell in New York to become 'the premier featherweight champion of the world'. A fairy story, ghetto to glory and so on – except that all Jim Driscoll got for his World Crown was a stint as an Army P T instructor in the First World War. No lifetime achievement awards made in his name, no books, and certainly no films.

But in these sport-saturated days, when games, fights and races, can be seen, replayed and interacted with from forty different angles and in super-slow-motion until we ought to be able to feel the straining muscles as if they were our own, we still need words to validate achievement. And more often than not those words come from second-hand car-dealer managers and promoters, who can add no deeper insight to the greatest comeback of all time, for example, than the 'game of two halves'. So, of all the achievements – the World Championship and the ill-fated comeback, the controversial fight with another Welsh World Champion, Freddie Welsh, and the 100,000 people who lined the streets of Cardiff on the day of his funeral – you get the feeling that being ignored by post-match 'analysis', and the whole culture of ready-made heroes, was, and is Jim Driscoll's greatest feat.

Owen Martell

GARETH EDWARDS

'This is the plan. When are the opposing wing-forwards least effective?'

'Mid-field, around the half-way mark.'

'Good! Wait for a scrum around that area if possible. Pick up the ball and, as quick as a flash, run towards the opposing outside-half, sell him a dummy, sidestep the full-back and score under the posts, OK?' I didn't realise the matter-of-fact way in which I was speaking.

'All right,' he said, with a grin on his face. This was a challenge, just between him and me. I had no doubt at all that he could accomplish the task; I was positive he could, for I was certain he had the skill, determination and speed to do it.

The Cardiff Rugby Club had adopted a very sensible method of invigilating their trial games. They dispersed their committee members at various locations around the pitch so that all the trialists were under close observation all the time.

I took his tracksuit and training shoes from him and, finally, said to him, 'Show these city types what the Welsh-speaking peasants of the Swansea Valley can do.' With that he went on the field.

A scrum-half cannot help but be in the picture straight away, but Gareth appeared quite harmless, fulfilling his role efficiently as a member of the team. When the opponents knocked on at the halfway line and a scrum formed, I could feel my pulse increasing its tempo. It was zero-hour.

Time to blow the fuse! Without showing any indication at all of going on his own, he executed the ploy with so much ease that one might have imagined the defending players changed into blocks of wood. The few spectators in attendance gave him a rousing applause. 'Scora un arall! Score another one!' I shouted to him in Welsh.

When the trial ended, some of the trialists realised that they had played in the company of a potential rugby genius and went to shake his hand. The committee members also appreciated the fact that they had witnessed an extraordinary young player, and converged on him from their various posts to shake the hand of a very shy young man. The genial character Stan Bowes, a pillar of the Cardiff club who is well known in the rugby world, came up to me and said, 'He promises to be the best West Walian ever,' which, coming from a stout Cardiffian like Stan, was indeed a compliment.

Bill Samuel

HUGH EDWARDS

'Jumbo' Edwards went up to Christ Church College, Oxford from Westminster School, and rowed in the Oxford boat as freshman in 1926 when his brother was also a member of the crew. Unfortunately, Edwards collapsed when the Dark Blues held a slight lead and Cambridge went on to win by five lengths.

In 1927, Edwards was rusticated for failing his examinations and he then spent two years as a schoolmaster, although he continued to row regularly with the London Rowing Club. While he was teaching, Edwards decided to follow his brother into the Royal Air Force, and the only avenue open to him by which he could secure a permanent commission was to return to Oxford and obtain a University degree. So in 1930, Edwards went back to Oxford, took his degree and then joined the RAF the following year. During his second period at Oxford, he devoted more time to flying than to rowing and obtained Proctorial

Licence No. 1, which enabled him to keep his private plane at the University. However, he was still good enough to command a place in the Oxford boat and five years after his first appearance he rowed again in the 1930 Boat Race. Referrring to the 1930 race, Edwards later wrote, 'I was incomparably the best oarsman in either crew', but apparently his Oxford colleagues could not match his talents as Cambridge won by two lengths.

Later in 1930, Edwards was in the London Rowing Club crew which won the Grand and the Stewards' at Henley and he then went to Canada for the British Empire Games, where he won gold medals in the coxless fours and the eights. In 1931, he won three events at Henley; the Grand, the Stewards' and the Goblets. At the 1932 Olympics he became only the second man in Olympic history to win two rowing gold medals on the same day. Firstly, he won the coxless pairs with Lewis Clive and then he was a member of the winning crew in the coxless fours, having been brought in as a late substitute for Thomas Tyler who contracted influenza after arriving in California. All these victories added up to a remarkable display of stamina for a man who had collapsed in the 1926 Boat Race.

After being commissioned into the RAF in 1931, Edwards became a well-known racing pilot and, in his own plane, finished second in the King's Cup of 1935. During the war, he served with Coastal Command, winning the AFC in 1943 and the DFC the following year. In 1943, his rowing ability literally saved his life. Being forced to ditch his Liberator off Land's End, he rowed a dinghy for four miles before getting clear of the minefield in which he had landed. He was the only survivor of his crew.

Group Captain Edwards retired from the RAF in 1946, and soon developed a reputation as an innovative coach. He advised his old University on a number of occasions, including 1959 when his son was in the Oxford crew, and he also coached Britain's Olympic eight in 1960.

Ian Buchanan
British Olympians — A Hundred Years of Gold Medallists
(Guinness)

ANNE ELLIS

'It doesn't matter if it's tiddly-winks; if you're representing Wales, you wear that red shirt with pride' How often I heard that declaration before a game and coming as it did from someone with such passion and commitment as Anne Ellis, you could not fail to be motivated to play your best.

The first time I saw Anne play hockey was at Stradey Park, when she represented her country against England. It was every young girl's dream in those days to play hockey or netball at international level. It was my privilege to play hockey for Wales and Great Britain with Anne as captain, and indeed, what an inspiration she proved to be both on and off the field. She was modest, caring, wise and totally focused on the job in hand.

Consistency was the hallmark of her game, and a testimony to her determination and resilience. Her 'never-say-die' attitude influenced her team mates; her kestrel-bright eyes led her into many scrapes and, more often than not, she came out on top. She resembled a heat-seeking missile; always in the thick of the action. At the end of every encounter, the smell of sweat rather than Chanel No. 5 permeated the changing room; you had to commit yourself totally for your club, country and for Anne Ellis. Nerves and sinews had to be stretched throughout the match; Anne would have it no other way.

As a player, her judgement was uncanny. She was cool and composed under pressure; a true professional in an amateur world. And when Anne Ellis lunged through from midfield, others had to react and do so in an instant.

After she retired from competitive hockey, Anne concentrated on coaching. As vice-chair of the Sports Council and President of the Welsh Hockey Association, Anne is still actively involved in all aspects of the game in Wales. Her enthusiasm is infectious and, while that remains, the future of Welsh sport is secure.

Marilyn Pugh

JOE ERSKINE

On most mornings, about half past eight or nine, you could see Joe, tidily attired in suit and tie and his wavy black hair slickly Brylcreemed, walking from the direction of Roath down to Bute Street and the Bay. There, in Bab's Bistro, he could enjoy an early beer before the pubs opened.

He was gentle mannered, sometimes overly polite and always effusively talkative. Unbeknown to him (I presume) among those who drank with him down the Bay and in the pubs on Broadway in Roath were some petty villains whose trade was trafficking in weapons for Cardiff's underworld – and some of these characters were far more sinister than anyone Joe faced in the boxing arena.

During his last years, his closest friend was the renowned old boxing trainer Jack Chambers – a Cardiff West Indian who more than once stood for Plaid Cymru in Adamsdown and Butetown. The only time I was warned to move out of Joe's way was by Jack Chambers at the end of a drunken evening in the Royal Oak pub in Splott. We were sitting in the little square back bar, and Joe was on a low stool wedged in one corner of the bar. 'This bar is exactly the same dimensions as a boxing ring,' said Jack . . . 'You and I are in the corner opposite Joe. He's staring over at us. And any minute now they're going to ring the bell for stop tap. I think we'd better move . . .'

In reality Joe wouldn't have lifted a finger to harm a fly. He was like some affable old bear, so keen was he to befriend and humour all those in his company.

He fought 54 bouts, winning 45, and he was the heavyweight champion of Britain between 1956 and 1958. In February 1990 he was found dead in his top floor flat in Moira Street, Adamsdown, where he lived alone and in relative poverty, following a second divorce some eighteen months previously.

Siôn Eirian

SIR CHARLES EVANS

Whichever way you look at it, it's a long way from the Berwyn mountains around Bala to the Himalayas in Nepal. However, it was a journey that Charles Evans undertook several times during his lifetime in order to savour the 'ultimate mountaineering experience'.

Born in the the Clwyd Valley, he was a neurologist by profession, and worked in this capacity at Walton Hospital in Liverpool. Such was his love of the mountains that he thought nothing of driving down from Liverpool on a cold Friday night in January after a busy day at the hospital to arrive at Pen-y-Gwryd at around ten o'clock. He would then make an assault on the mountains in the dead of night when the only light available was the moonlight reflected off the snow. After a few hours sleep, he would drive back to Liverpool to begin another day on the wards.

All this experience stood him in good stead when he was chosen as the deputy leader of the successful expedition which conquered Everest in 1953. He was one of the first in the group to attempt the assault on the summit, but unfortunately had to give up when only three hours from the top because of problems with his oxygen equipment.

Nothing dampened his enthusiasm for the mountains and a head injury sustained during an attempt to save a fellow climber was pointedly disregarded as a minor irritation.

One tragedy that could not be ignored, however, was the multiple sclerosis which was diagnosed when he was only 39 years old. For such an active individual to have to spend the next 25 years of his life in a wheelchair was indeed a cruel blow.

In his latter years, Charles Evans was appointed Principal of the University of North Wales, Bangor from 1958, until ill health forced him to retire in 1984. This period of his life was not without controversy, as several of his policy-making decisions were hugely unpopular with staff and students alike. But he did not yield to pressure from any quarter, and until the end his only means of escape was his beloved mountains.

Nêst Roberts

Portrait by
Sir Kyffin Williams.

43

EDGAR EVANS

On the 17th of February 1912, Petty Officer Edgar Evans died a hero on the return journey from a successful visit to the South Pole. Circumstances beyond his control led to his burial in the frozen wastes, far from his Welsh home.

Edgar Evans was born in Rhosili, which at that time was a remote village at the furthest extremity of the Gower Peninsula, with a small population which consisted mainly of farmers, weavers and millers. Evans joined the Royal Navy and rose through the ranks to become a Petty Officer (non-commissioned officer) and had, prior to the 1910-1912 Expedition, been a member of the 'Discovery' team of 1901-1904. All who describe him in their reports speak of a 'big, broad, sinewy Welshman'. Ponting says that P. O. Edgar 'Taff' Evans was the 'strong man' of the Pole Party.

We have to read Captain Scott's diary of the trek to the Pole, and the disastrous return, to learn how they all perished. The Expedition left Cardiff in 1910, and after an eighteen-month struggle in a hostile environment, the Pole party, comprising Captain Scott, Dr. Wilson, Captain Oates and P. O. Evans, left the support party at 87 deg. 32 mins. South to commence the final 800 miles to the Pole. Evans had the immense responsibility of maintaining the sledge equipment.

They reached the South Pole on 16th January, 1912, only to find that Amundsen and his Norwegian party had reached the Pole first using dog sledges. Then commenced the horrific return journey outlined in Scott's diary. All suffered terribly from the cold and starvation, in addition to the burden of towing the sledges through difficult terrain. Modern leaders can identify the factors that led to the heroic deaths of Evans and the others. Firstly, the unwise decision to use horses and men instead of dogs caused problems and, secondly, an inadequate diet resulted in vitamin deficiency.

Evans had the additional psychological problem of being the only non-officer and of belonging to a completely different social class and culture from his companions. The strain of sharing a small tent with such 'remote' officers and being expected to be the 'strong man' must have been intolerable for the brave Welshman. He died exhausted and confused on the 16th February 1912, and was buried alongside the others who perished.

In Rhosili Church there is a white marble memorial tablet erected by his widow, Lois Evans. Inscribed on this tablet are the very appropriate words from Tennyson's 'Ulysses', 'To seek, to strive, to find and not to yield'.

Ken Maddocks

GWYNDAF EVANS

My first contact with Gwyndaf Evans was in the '80s when as a sports broadcaster I was asked to film an up-and-coming rally driver from North Wales. Initially I was suspicious, not because he ran a garage in Dolgellau, as you might expect, but what made me wonder was the fact that Gwyndaf also drove the local school bus! Can you imagine – this was manna from heaven for a journalist, and had to be checked out. And it was indeed completely true. Gwyndaf proved to be

a most modest, shy and unassuming person in complete contrast to the high octane atmosphere of a rally. But his calm and quiet disposition has enabled him to climb to the top of his profession, ably assisted by his navigator Howard Davies. He quickly realised that possessing driving abilities of the highest order may not be enough, but you also have to be aware of the needs of the media in this high publicity sport. Gwyndaf is also bilingual which increases the demands made upon him in this respect. I will never forget the drive from Gwyndaf's home in Dinas Mawddwy to his garage in Dolgellau in his normal road car. I was a front seat passenger and Gwyndaf chatted away as he effortlessly guided the car through the twists and turns of the winding road with just a turn of the steering wheel here and there, with me glued to the seat! He has competed in world championships rallies all over the world. However when I asked him where he would choose to live of all the places he'd visited, his reply was immediate and delivered in his quiet yet sure voice 'Right here in Dinas Mawddwy – there's nowhere like it in the World!'

Owen Jenkins

IEUAN EVANS

Grace under pressure is a dictum that could always be applied to Ieuan Evans, whatever the environment, whatever the circumstance. On the inside there was ebullient passion, whether he was playing for Llanelli, Wales or the Lions, but rarely was that fire allowed to run out of his control even in the most desperate of circumstances or under the most extreme provocation.

One try encapsulated that mixture of iron determination, exquisite skill and unflappable temperament. It may not have been his most memorable score or one that is always replayed on television, but it said as much about the man as any he scored for club or country.

Having failed to make the knockout stages of the 1991 World Cup, Wales had been forced to qualify for the 1995 tournament. Victories over Spain and Portugal had ensured their place, but they still had to travel to Bucharest to play Romania in order to determine seeding.

It was September 1994. In a crumbling 60,000 capacity stadium that was less than a tenth full, a struggling Wales were trailing to a workmanlike Romanian side whose main advantage was familiarity with autumn temperatures of over 80 degrees. Despite suffering from a stomach upset and dehydration, Ieuan Evans rose above the mediocrity around him by scoring a try out of nothing to turn the game.

Released by a Rupert Moon pass, he used his speed, strength and cunning to weave a pattern to the tryline – something his team mates looked incapable of managing, had they played all day. As he crossed the line, he was assaulted by a petulant Romanian's late tackle. It was a pointless act which served only to remind one of Evans's powers of self-restraint, and allowed Neil Jenkins to re-start with a successsful penalty kick from halfway.

It also happened to be the try which put Evans's name into the record books as the leading Welsh try-scorer of all time. From the back of the press box, one man stood to applaud generously. He was Gerald Davies, whose record had just been taken.

Graham Thomas

MALDWYN LEWIS EVANS

His sport was one which seemed boring and monotonous to his fellow pupils but which captured the imagination of Maldwyn Lewis Evans. However, the family influence proved crucial, especially that of his father. His contribution as mentor, coach and friend was vital. Maldwyn's brother, uncle and son represented Wales – an unique achievement.

According to Maldwyn, 'Every bowler's success is totally dependant on his or her local bowling club.' He represented Gelli Park from the 50s to the present day and during the 60s and 70s the club dominated the national bowls scene. Its influence and success were quite remarkable. The Welsh Championship was won four times, and the club came second on two occasions, with eight of the club's players being chosen to represent Wales.

1964 was an important milestone for Maldwyn. He was chosen to represent his country for the first time and proved an inspirational performer during the next fifteen seasons. He played in the World Championships at Sydney, Australia in 1966, winning the copper medal (a medal presented to those finishing fourth in such prestigious championships). In this particular competition, Maldwyn was the only individual to defeat David Bryant, one of the sport's greatest ever competitors.

Maldwyn's finest achievement was winning the gold medal in the World Championships at Worthing in 1972. Previous champions, young upstarts, seasoned campaigners – all these had to step aside as Evans truly excelled; his consistency, vision and all-round play paid dividends as the Welshman crowned a glorious career by claiming the winner's medal. A dream had been realised. He represented Wales around the globe, the Commonwealth Games included. He retired from competitive bowls in 1976 after competing in the World Championships in South Africa.

A brain tumour and stomach cancer were the reasons behind his premature retirement. However, his determination and unquenchable spirit paved the way for a truly incredible recovery. The do-or-die attitude and positive approach which had conquered so many on the bowling greens around the world aided his recovery. He is still to be seen drawing the wood to within a hair's breadth of the Jack amidst his colleagues in the Rhondda Valleys. Maldwyn Lewis Evans is held in high esteem in the village of Ton Pentre – a legend in his own community, and his achievement in winning forty major championships is testimony to his ability.

Maldwyn is still to be seen coaching and encouraging young bowlers who intend to make a mark in the world of bowls. He is a national selector able to look back on his career with a sense of pride; challenging the best and occasionally proving victorious.

Alan Thomas

TOMMY FARR

Tommy Farr is a folk hero, Tommy Farr swaggers modestly, Tommy Farr is resilient, and he fights hard and often before gaining any recognition by the boxing fraternity.

On August 30th, 1937, he fought Joe Louis. That was his key contest when he gained a moral victory, if not a technical one, and his failure was a glorious one.

Thus Farr is Tommy's autobiography, which he wrote years ago and which was allowed to lie dormant until it was unearthed and edited by his son Gary. It opens with a provocative essay entitled 'A Pugilist's Philosophy'. His cliché-free cameos depicting the prize fighter's lot are clearly drawn and laden with wisdom and guilt gained during more than twenty years in and around the 'roped cage'.

'At the age of 12,' he says, 'I had my first fight, and at 40 I had my last. At any time I could have quit the ring but never did. They threw me in and they threw me out, and in all the years between there was never a whimper. It served me well and it served me right.'

After quitting the local pit, he served for a while as a kitchen help, a waiter of sorts, a furniture remover and a fireman on a Thames garbage boat. Then, who should come on the scene but Jobby Churchill, a truly remarkable man who, after losing a leg whilst working underground, had set himself up as a saddler. He became Farr's mentor and remained so until the end of 1937. Once Jobby's advice was ignored, the dice turned against Farr.

It was in Joe Gess's boxing booth at Tylorstown that he took up the fight game proper and it proved a hard slog from then until 1937 and his high water mark. The Farr versus Louis fight is covered in the most revealing and interesting chapters in the book. Against the wishes of Jobby and Ted Broadribb, his manager, Farr got himself sucked into America and committed himself to Mike Jacobs, the all-powerful boxing mogul. All the time, he was tasting too deeply of the good things of life, and there was no one around to remind him of his foolishness.

Farr sidesteps some important issues and details as adroitly as he parried his opponents' best shots. Ill health hastens his first retirement, and various business

Tommy Farr (left) fighting to the bitter end against Joe Louis.

ventures in Brighton fail. Following a candid chapter, 'The Last Phase' by Gary Farr the editor, Tommy appropriately gets the last word with his final chapter entitled 'Why I Am Coming Back?'

Thus Farr is an ideal gift, not only for the over-60 boxing enthusiast, but also for all those who remain adamant that things are not what they used to be, and that Tommy Farr was unquestionably the best heavyweight we ever had.

Moc Rogers

TREVOR FORD

A Saturday evening in winter in our little terraced house in Abertyswg, a small coal-mining village at the top of the Rhymney valley, was definitely the time for discussion. Equipped with the football results from *Sports Report* on the wireless, and the pink pages of the *Football Echo*, we digested the football (and rugby) fixtures of the day. I supported Cardiff City – Cardiff was a distant metropolis, and to me synonymous with Trevor Ford. Ford was definitely a colliers' football player, as his physical strength and hard determination on the field were a mirror image of the coal miners of my youth in the West Monmouthshire coalfield. Ford was a necessary hero who brought colour to the grey years of low wages and the demeaning politics of deprivation.

He was a Swansea boy, the son of a manager of the Townhill cinema. After a brief forging period at Townhill Steelworks, he signed professional forms for Swansea in 1942. Thus began a career of leading the line, always wearing the number 9 shirt as if it was his birthright, the young player, volatile and opinionated, signed for Aston Villa in 1947, before joining Sunderland three years later for a fee of £50,000. At that time he was the most expensive footballer in the world. However, he did not really settle in the North East of England, and in 1953 he and his family were relieved to return to Wales when he signed for Cardiff.

Now the most talked about player in the British Isles, Ford was at his peak, and was the main attraction for 25,000 supporters who packed into Ninian Park to watch mid-week games.

Dark and swarthy in appearance, Trevor Ford was dramatically committed to the red national shirt, and won the first of his 28 caps in 1948. He scored consistently, with both feet, and was the terror of international goalkeepers from the Atlantic coast to the Balkans, as he hit scorching goals into his opponents' net with consistent ferocity. His gladiatorial style of play sent ball and goal-keeper hurtling into the net; he was the most combative centre-forward of his generation.

51

Ford was also combative off the field, and became increasingly willing to express his views in newspaper articles. Unfit footballers who drank too much, corrupt and dictatorial club directors – these were the ripe targets harpooned by the Trevor Ford missiles in the 1950s.

And then Cardiff City was on the gradient of decline. Ford ended his major playing days with PSV Eindhoven, in The Netherlands, before suffering the bad injury which had been awaiting such a ferocious player. After a short spell in exile with minor league English clubs he was back in Swansea and back in Wales. In September 1999, Ford underwent surgery for a replacement knee.

Trevor Ford was the most colourful and dramatic player ever to lead the line for Wales; a bright beacon in a very murky era; an unfashionable radical dissenter in soccer politics.

Astra Thomas

SCOTT GIBBS

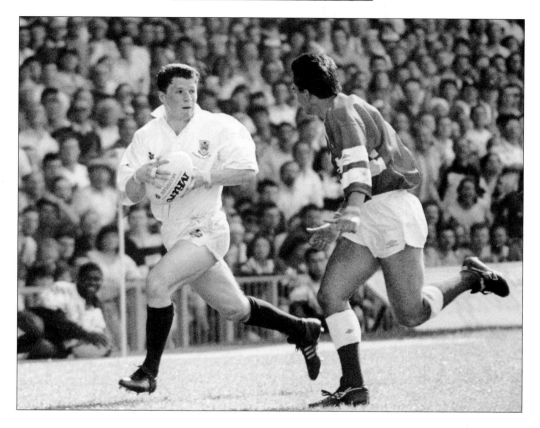

It was once said of Scott Gibbs that he had a problem with direction: he knew exactly where to go on the pitch, but he didn't have a clue where to head off it.

Those were the days when Gibbs agonised over whether to switch to rugby league from union, the period in his life when he could not make up his mind whether to stay in Wales and make the best of a package of business contracts, or move north to take the rugby league shilling.

His indecision was final. Stay in Wales? Maybe. Turn Pro? Possibly. No fence proved too high for the centre to climb on.

Seven years on it is hard to imagine a more direct person than Gibbs.

On the field his spear-like thrusts have inspired dread among opposition centres. No defence is too solid for the triple British Lion to go through.

Off the pitch, his straight-talking suggests a player who knows his own mind. No longer are issues clouded in doubt.

Rugby is a professional sport and Gibbs is the ultimate professional. He trains hard, plays hard, takes his money and goes home.

It is an approach encapsulated in a remark he made before the test with Italy in October 1996, when he became the first rugby league returnee to regain his place in the Wales team. 'History does not mean much to me. I just want to play and pick up my win bonus,' he declared. It was a stark comment that jarred with many and evoked memories of Swansea chairman Mike James branding Gibbs a 'rugby prostitute' after the former Neath player left for the 13-a-side code. But it is too harsh to brand Gibbs a mercenary. He is simply a modern-day player who gives good value for his services.

His time in rugby is already littered with memorable events, from winning a first cap just 15 games into his senior career to scoring the injury-time try that handed Wales their dramatic 1999 victory over England. In his third season as Swansea captain, he is now more mature and focused. He knows where he is going and what it takes to get there. His blunt personality divides opinion like he divides defences. But he is one player Wales could not have been without.

Mark Orders

RYAN GIGGS

Just before the World Cup of 1998 we were dining in a hotel in London. On the next table to us there were some rowdy businessmen discussing the competition and its outstanding players. 'I'll tell you something,' said the loudest, 'the best player in the world isn't even playing.' My husband warned me under his breath not to interject, but too late! Ryan Giggs's name slipped over my lips as naturally as breathing. The men looked mutely in my direction. 'He's Welsh,' I bragged, 'and I'm glad you agree that a Welshman is the best player in the world.'

For the rest of the evening, his name resounded like a bell in my head, and if I knew his phone number I would have rung him. Not that he needs my praises. He does not strike me as a big-headed, look-at-me type, nor is he a player to cause trouble through foul-playing. And why should he when his feet do the talking for him? He is the swallow of the playing field. The ball seems to be attached to his left foot like a horizontal yo-yo. There is no greater sight in the world game than Giggs careering down the left wing dribbling a golden path through a defence to plant the ball in the back of the net.

After the famous goal Giggs scored against Arsenal in the semi-final replay of the FA Cup in 1999, Alex Ferguson said that he shone like a genius among giants. Some call that goal the goal of the century. It will be shown again and again, immortalising Giggs's talent and that of Welsh football. That businessman in the hotel in London was spot-on when he said that you don't have to belong to one of the bigger countries to be the best player of your generation.

Jane Edwards

TERRY GRIFFITHS

I don't recall or much care who won the World Professional Snooker title at the Crucible in 1997 – all that sticks in my mind is a poignant image of Terry Griffiths, bespectacled and immaculately attired, hair just so, walking away from the brightly lit green baize arena to the darkness of the exit curtains for the last time. Under his left arm is the black cue case, his trusty cue in his left hand and his right arm is raised high acknowledging the crowd's thunderous applause for a departing all-time great. This proud son of Llanelli was probably humming Sospan Fach one more time as he struggled to keep his Celtic emotions in check.

A recently published list of all-time money winners in snooker had our Terry in sixth position with earnings of over £1.4 million. Not bad for a misspent youth as the old saw has it! Much easier than being a postie or insurance collector, that's for certain.

Much of his deserved financial success (totally deserved through great technique, skill and a champion's temperament) has been earned in our living room whilst the snooker boom of the late 70s and 80s swept all beside it away on colour television. A long way from the one-frame Pot Black tournaments: that wasn't a programme that would have suited Terry's careful, thoughtful analysis and approach. More for your hurricanes and whirlwinds perhaps. But softly softly catchee monkey indeed.

South Wales was buzzing in 1979; Mr Toshack's Swans were swooping upwards towards ever more dizzying heights each season, Welsh rugby was drawing a golden era to a close and in Sheffield, of all places, a young slim blond chap was turning the established snooker world on its head. It all made for powerful and essential TV viewing. Patient and risk free, liberally dosed with audacious and consistent potting, silently humming and whistling his way into legend, raising an eyebrow now and then if things went awry, Terry took it one careful step at a time. After all, he was on the threshold of greatness.

The darkness, the brightly lit table, penguin-like referees with white gloves, brilliantined like Dennis Compton, traditional stocky men with short back and sides took on upstarts with longer locks and flared trousers. A new wave had arrived, and the stiff backed Perrie Mans, Fred Davis and steady Eddie Charlton were being swept away. Down the Vetch Field there were huge roars when Terry's latest break and frame scores were announced over the tannoy. Forget *Match of the Day* and Jimmy Hill, that night we'd be glued to BBC2, David Vine and whispering Ted Lowe.

Our shattered but happy hero announced to the stay-awakes at home in the early hours after a tensely fought match, 'A lot of people still here at two in the morning!!' His twinkly eyes, Welsh sing-song drawl and mop of hair endeared him to the nation.

Final day, and the other Celtic hero Dennis Taylor lay between Terry and a debut World title. Could he dare dream the impossible dream? Could he sense the Stradey-like fervour of thousands of Welsh supporters both in the arena and at home willing him to walk with the gods? 24 frames to 16 and the title is heading for Llanelli and Wales. Haleliwia!!!! Mam fach, he's done it, YEEEEEESSSS!!!!! Watch out Ray Reardon, the new gun's for hire. Why he even knocked rugby off the back page of the *Western Mail*!

Defeated Dennis would earn his moment in the sun when pinching the black and title versus superman Steve Davis in the future, but Terry was a most deserving champion and his long successful career has shown his character and perseverance. 1988, another World final, but fellow matchroom pal Steve was in his pomp and it was not to be, but Terry accepted his defeat with grace and bonhomie as ever. Finally, in 1997, as our Terry walked away from the Crucible for the last time, the hiraeth and memories came flooding back. He'd stood on top of Everest and no one could take that feeling away ever again.

Phil Davies

CHRIS HALLAM

Chris Hallam has been one of the most successful and prolific athletes in the history of Welsh sport. He has been the epitome of determination and fortitude, overcoming his disability in a manner seldom matched in any sphere of society.

His tragic and unfortunate motor cycle accident two days before he was to compete in the Senior Welsh Swimming trials would have meant for most people a retreat within themselves but Chris was not distracted from his lifelong ambition of achieving the highest accolades in sport. Misfortune instilled in him an energy and a commitment to succeed that has seldom been replicated and, within a mere two years of his accident, he began his career as a top-class paraplegic sportsman.

He has distinguished himself both as a swimmer and a wheelchair racer. Success in swimming includes gold medals at the 1984 Olympics and the 1986 World Championships and setting a world record during the World Championships.

One of the main reasons that Chris took an interest in the London Marathon was because of the enormous media exposure that the wheelchair event received. He wanted greater exposure for disabled sportsmen and women and felt that success at this event would bring awareness to a World audience. He achieved his goal!

This example simply reinforces the fact that Chris Hallam has always subordinated his own abilities to the demands of others and the organisations that promote disabled sport in all its facets.

Chris's attitude, demeanour and endeavour give him that extra 'life force' that has led to enormous achievement and sporting prowess. 'Chris Hallam is one of those truly unquenchable human beings within whom the flame of life burns brightly.'

John M. Pugh

JUDGE ROWE HARDING

There is a select band of Welsh players of truly outstanding ability who had the bad luck to feature in eras when the National XV failed to deliver consistent success.

In this context, the career of Ieuan Evans springs to mind. Though World War II interrupted his career, Tanner is also in this category. Going back further, big Wick Powell is with him. And, most certainly, his brilliant contemporary Rowe Harding belongs there too.

The Gowerton Grammar School product, four times a Cambridge Blue, won 17 Welsh caps on the wing between 1923 and 1928, yet played in only one victory over a Home Country – Ireland. Two Wooden Spoons came Wales's way in his time.

Harding was also unlucky with injuries, as a broken collarbone and, later, a torn hamstring cost him three or four more caps.

There can be no doubting his quality, however. All the match reports testify to the blistering speed which was a factor in his selection for the 1924 British Isles tour of South Africa, where he played in three Tests.

As a barrister and ultimately a Judge, he nonetheless made time to serve his club Swansea nobly in later life, as well as becoming chairman of Glamorgan County Cricket Club.

I was privileged to meet Rowe at the snug villa on Gower where he spent his last years. The visit was for a specific purpose – to record on camera his predictions concerning the latest match between the All Whites and New Zealand.

But my vivid memory is of his desire to talk on, long after the TV crew had gone. At the time, one of the periodic debates about professionalism was taking place – exchanges that obsessed Wales in times that now seem mediaeval.

While avoiding pros and cons, I argued that professionalism would come, because of player-pressure and the inevitability of change. The Judge bowed his head, noble but austere.

Then he looked up. 'You must permit my view,' he said evenly. 'The amateur player puts rugby in a special category, as a pursuit in which the game is its own reward. Those who play it seek no other – save that of belonging to a unique and special brotherhood.'

It was a handsome statement, spoken from the heart rather than the head.

But that is how true amateurs once felt and spoke. Even though circumstances have rendered such views dated, we should not forget that the vast – yes, vast – majority of those who play rugby do so for the motives cited by Rowe Harding.

David Parry Jones

ROBERT HOWLEY

The tour of Australia by the 2001 Lions ended in failure, and Robert Howley played just two of the three tests. The prevailing feeling when the party arrived home was one of severe let down because the Lions really should have won. Howley, no doubt, shared the feeling of deflation. However, there is absolutely no doubt in my mind that in the season 2000-01 which ended with the tour, Howley finally secured his place in history as one of the all-time great Welsh players. I thought that he had a majestic season. He was always under pressure, always having to prove himself whilst playing for mediocre sides. But he was a jewel.

Howley began the international season by making a nonsense of the idea that England's defence was impregnable, scoring one superb try and creating another. His 80-metre dash for a try against France in Paris was heroic. From a distance, it was just an initial break followed by an eyeballs-out sprint. Look closer, and you see all kinds of swerves and changes of pace, made in order to convince the French defence that he intended to pass.

Howley on the Lions tour was operating at a level higher than any other scrum-half of the season and of recent seasons. It was also a demonstration of all the arts. His service was superb. Before the tour began, he was in competition for the test position from Matt Dawson and Austin Healey. However well the two Englishmen played, though, the difference in the speed and accuracy of pass when they were pitted against each was marked.

Howley's box-kicking and other kicking was excellent, and he made breaks which were rationed and therefore highly-effective. His tactical mastery was complete. Perhaps above all, he was cool under pressure. He was teak-tough, but he was able to play as if he alone had time, whereas everyone else seemed to be in a tearing rush.

He missed the final test due to injury. However, if you had seen at close quarters Howley's grief at being injured before the test series in the 1997 Lions tour, when he was playing brilliantly; or if you had suffered with him when he lost form and the sympathy of Graham Henry in 1999, then you would not feel that Howley has unfinished business.

Stephen Jones

BRIAN HUGGETT

If any golfer can lay claim to having put Wales on the world golfing map, then surely Brian Huggett could do so. The 'Welsh bulldog' as he became affectionately known following his inspirational captaincy of the Great Britain Ryder Cup team in 1977, not only had a slight facial resemblance to that symbol of British resilience in times of war, but also played his golf the same way!

Runner-up in the Open championship in 1965, and with 15 tournament victories to his name until the arrival on the scene of Ian Woosnam, Brian, along with Dai Rees, was the most influential and charismatic Welsh golfer of the post-war period.

Brian was a fervent supporter of other Welsh sports and sportsmen. During my days as a professional cricketer with Glamorgan, Brian was a regular visitor to our dressing room at away matches; at the time he was living in Cambridgeshire. He was fascinated by the technical and physical demands made by our game and marvelled at what he perceived was the kind of mental courage we needed to face the likes of Frank Tyson, Fred Trueman and Brian Statham. In return, we golfers in the team marvelled at his ability to hit the ball so far and straight and knock it close to the pin from elephant-high rough!

Besides his formidable playing track record, Brian has been responsible for designing a number of new golf courses in the UK, which in time will become classics. At the height of his playing career Brian was, and indeed still is, a sponsor or corporate day client's dream, unfailingly courteous and never short of an encouraging word of advice or a technical tip.

Although for the past fifteen years he's lived in England on the outskirts of Ross-on-Wye, he remains, as ever, a fiercely proud Welshman. That was exemplified recently on September 28th 2001 when the announcement confirming Wales's Ryder Cup appointment was made – Brian Huggett was just over the moon'.

Peter Walker

MARK HUGHES

In terms of Welsh football, Mark Hughes has been something of a colossus during his long and illustrious career.

His footballing talents have seen him play for some of Europe's finest clubs – Manchester United (twice), Barcelona, Bayern Munich, Chelsea, Southampton and now Blackburn. During this time he has assumed a legendary status that few Welsh sportsmen have achieved during their lifetimes. Winning over 70 caps for Wales, being the first player this century to play in four winning FA Cup teams and securing championship and Cup Winners Cup medals are testimony to his huge success as a player.

His array of skills in a domestic game that has been wonderfully enriched in recent years by foreign talent have remained undiminished – a great passer of a ball, a fine header and superb volleyer, a ferocious tackler with an ability to shield the ball with the durability of an armadillo. Added to this is that something that can only be bestowed, and not honed on a practice pitch – an intimidating presence that puts the fear of God into opposing defenders. It's that Jonah Lomu factor that makes grown men quiver.

That Mark Hughes is no shrinking violet is a mischievous understatement. His abundant collection of yellow and red cards is a graphic illustration of a style of play based on passion and absolute commitment. His single-mindedness, determination, bravery and willingness to 'mix it' with some of the game's renowned 'hard men' are traits more akin to the Celtic warriors of bygone days who considered a few cuts and bruises the well-earned medals of honour. His trademark competitive spirit means that he could bite your leg but make no bones about it, receive a whack on the nose and get on with the game unperturbed.

Not for him the petulant tantrums, histrionics and exaggerated play-acting of some of his more excitable colleagues, but a no-frills appreciation of the rough and tumble world of professional football.

The image that he conjures up is one that makes a caricaturist's pen convulse with joy – legs like tree trunks, neck muscles that put a pit bull terrier to shame, elbows flailing in the penalty box and the guts of a kamikaze bungee jumper.

When one thinks of Mark Hughes, one automatically thinks of spectacular goals like the brilliant over-head volley against Spain at the Racecourse in 1985, the rocket into the roof of the net after cleverly rounding the goalkeeper in the European Cup Winners Cup Final in Rotterdam in 1991 when Man United beat Barcelona 2-1, and his last-minute equaliser against Oldham in the semi-final of the FA Cup in 1994 which kept United's double hopes alive – a feat which they would achieve for the first time in their history.

Like many gifted sportsmen, the exterior persona often exudes a confidence that is in stark contrast to the off-stage character. Off the pitch, Mark Hughes is a quietly spoken and articulate young man who is able to express his thoughts in a concise and deliberate manner which reflects a refreshing sincerity and honesty in a sport which is prone to hyperbole and well-worn cliches.

His recent move from player to international manager has been as effortless as a glancing-back post-header. His relative success in such a short period of time reflects the huge amount of respect he attracts from fellow professionals who universally admire his utmost dedication and commitment.

To me, Mark Hughes has epitomised in his play the determination, courage and deep-rooted passion of the Welsh people in the most sublime way. He has been a great leader of men who has inspired others to follow. Of all the players who have worn the red shirt of Wales in recent years, none has espoused the spirit of Owain Glyndŵr more than the Wrexham-born braveheart whose spark will hopefully kindle the flames of Welsh footballing success for many years to come.

Cefin Campbell

COLIN JACKSON

Since the age of fourteen, Colin Jackson has dedicated his life to sporting excellence in one of the most exacting athletic disciplines, the 110 metre hurdles. That commitment, combined with great natural ability and a rare competitive spirit, has produced breathtaking performances and results.

World Champion, World Record Holder, Olympic Silver, Commonwealth Gold (twice), the list of titles and championships won is testimony to a truly great athlete. Sporting abilities tend to run in families and I once asked Ossie, Colin's dad, where he thought Colin's great ability came from. ' From me, man, from me,' he replied in his distinct Jamaican lilt, roaring with laughter. Ossie had been a very good all-round sportsman, reaching the all-Jamaican schools championships in cricket and football before emigrating to Britain in the late 50s.

Colin's sister Susanne, who is now a well-known television actress, was also a fine hurdler, setting schools and club records when she ran for Cardiff. Over the years I have come to know Colin very well. In temperament, as well as athletic ability, he is also like his dad; happy, easy-going, smiling, great sense of humour, enjoys a good laugh, uncomplicated. Angela, his mum, is the same and they are a very close family living together in a lovely home on the outskirts of Cardiff.

Colin loves Wales and he describes Cardiff as a 'wicked place'. It's his favourite expression for something he really rates. He recently received an Honorary Fellowship from the University of Wales Institute Cardiff (UWIC) at St David's Hall. Dr John Pugh, Dean of the Faculty of Education and Sport at UWIC compared him to a fine wine: 'He has depth, richness, character, complexity, blend and after taste.'

Athletics is a sport for individuals and success is down to that individual, but

Colin would be the first to acknowledge his coach and mentor, Malcolm Arnold, the former National Coach for Wales. He met Colin as a schoolboy and guided his career, planning his training and preparation. Over the years the coach/athlete relationship changes and matures, and now they are great friends still working together, with Malcolm fine-tuning Colin's well established skills and technique.

Last year, Colin mentioned in conversation that he was taking up the Long Jump, and I spent some time helping him in his training. He has all the qualities to be a very good long jumper; speed, balance, power and agility, and if he had persisted I have no doubt that he would have beaten my thirty-year-old British record of 8.23 metres. Fortunately, he decided to concentrate on hurdling and my record is safe for a few more years!

In the 1980s athletics enjoyed a golden era of international success, attracting wide television coverage and sponsorship. Colin, together with the likes of Linford Christie, Steve Cram, Sally Gunnell and Jonathan Edwards, has reaped financial rewards, which have provided him with security for life.

'A gold medal at Sydney would have been a tremendous way of topping my career but I'm already proud of my achievements and of what I've done for Wales,' he said recently. To which may be added, 'and Wales is proud of Colin Jackson, super athlete and great ambassador.'

Lynn Davies

STEVE JAMES

Over the past few years, there have been hordes of cricketers drafted into the England side for one or two caps. Glamorgan's Steve James is probably unique that his two call-ups were both barely twenty-four hours before the start of a Test, and were long overdue.

Educated at Monmouth School, Steve James made his first-class debut for Glamorgan at the end of the 1985 season, but never got onto the field, as rain washed out the match with Sussex. By the time of his next appearance in 1987, James was reading Classics at Swansea University, before taking a postgraduate course at Cambridge University.

Indeed, it was at Cambridge that Steve developed both a close friendship and an opening partnership with Mike Atherton. For many years, the Lancastrian had been destined for greater honours, but James lost little in comparison, and a match winning 131 against the 1990 New Zealanders bore testimony to James's class.

In 1992 James became Hugh Morris's regular opening partner in the Glamorgan side, and the pair added 250 against Lancashire at Colwyn Bay. They subsequently became a most prolific, and consistent, pairing in Championship matches, with James amongst the country's leading run-scorers. In 1996, James recorded a career best of 235 against Nottinghamshire at Worksop, and between 1996 and 1998 he amassed 4809 runs at an average of 55.92. Steve's 309 against Sussex at Colwyn Bay in the 2000 season was the highest ever individual score by a Glamorgan player.

At a time when many of the recognised England batsmen were failing, there were calls to promote the Glamorgan right-hander. It was James's sheer volume of runs that eventually led to his call-up to Test duty when Mark Butcher had to withdraw from the Second Test at Lord's against the 1998 Springboks. Later in the summer, he was called up on the eve of the one-off Test against Sri Lanka at The Oval when Atherton pulled out with a back injury. Once again, James had little time to gather his thoughts – more so, since his pregnant wife Jane had just gone into labour in Cardiff. His second cap may have been long overdue, but by the end of the Test, Steve was the proud father of Bethan.

Andrew Hignell

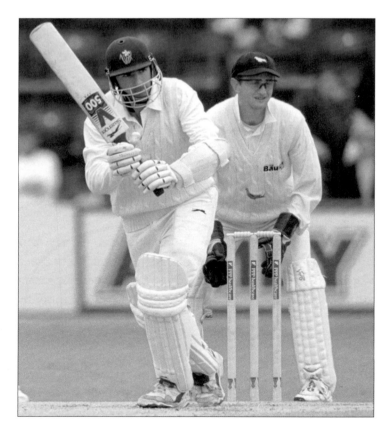

ALBERT JENKINS

Llanelli 1928 – Albert Jenkins, second from right, in the back row.

Albert Jenkins was corporate property. He belonged to the community, where he was known as 'Albert' from the highest to the humblest. Like so many sons of Stradey, he was often a Samson shorn when he crossed the Llwchwr river. On the Llanelli side of it, he was dynamite.

He could take a game into his own hands. Against Ireland in 1920 he dropped a goal, kicked two conversions, scored a try and made another three for his club partner Bryn Williams. Against Scotland in 1921 he broke the defence time and again only to see his efforts squandered by his outsides. With Scotland 11- 0 up, he began to bombard the Scottish posts with a ferocious barrage of pot-shots and kicks. He dropped two goals to bring Wales within three points, but then had to go off (the stories of Albert the mighty drinker who downed eight pints before a game, to retire briefly during the course of it with a strategic injury, were myths such as only legendary figures generate).

Only once was he knocked out, when tackled in scoring a try against Cardiff. The tackler was Jim Sullivan, and he was knocked out too, for trying to stop one of Albert's thirty-yard bursts was to invite concussion. At 5 foot 8 inches and 12.5 stone, his barrel chest and squat, stocky frame made him look shorter than he was, but those muscle-packed proportions tapered down to a sprinter's calves, narrow ankles and small, balletic feet. No ballet dancer, though, could have tackled like Albert. Blood coursed at the sight of him forcing a whole opposing three-quarter across field, until the luckless winger received both the ball and Albert simultaneously, and was deposited halfway up the bank.

On Saturday afternoons, long queues formed outside the gates of Stradey, to have the opportunity merely to carry the great man's bag. If it were rumoured that Albert was not playing, hundreds retraced their steps away from the ground. It was one of the great idiocies of the decade that Albert Jenkins won only fourteen caps.

David Smith / Gareth Williams
Fields of Praise
University of Wales Press

NEIL JENKINS

Most people judge Neil Jenkins coldly, objectively and mistakenly by the statistics that amass in his wake as his career ticks over with metronomic precision. Those who have moved in closer circles in his home-town club of Pontypridd, the club which nurtured him, know of other and deeper aspects to this sporting soul.

A mere points machine he is not. He is a highly skilled outside-half, a superb distributor, a creative support player and a courageous defender who can use his tactical awareness to the best effect at the best opportunity. He is also a proud and enthusiastic person whose resolve has been hardened in the white hot glare of a hostile media. The pundits grudgingly sang his praises as Neil won games for Wales and the Lions putting him on a precarious pedestal. They then took great delight in knocking him down as the national cause floundered through no fault of his own.

It's no coincidence that his former club, Pontypridd, are also classed as 'unfashionable', earning respect the hard way on the Welsh club circuit with a trench mentality based on a fierce valleys pride. Neil, like other icons before him, wore the club badge on his heart and wore it with a burning, often boyish, fervour.

Neil is an enigmatic figure. He could often be seen walking the corridors of the Ponty club, a pied piper figure, leading a motley band of friends, some less able than himself, being physically and mentally impaired. He will always take the cause of the underdog sensing, maybe, that he will always be one himself.

No matter what success and cult status may bring to this unassuming valleys boy, this hero will always have a corner to fight from. This rebel will always have a cause.

Guto Davies

BARRY JOHN

Nijinsky, Michelangelo, Muhammed Ali, Galileo Galilei, Edmund Hillary, William Shakespeare, Johan Cruyff, The Great Wall of China, Enrico Caruso, Aristotle, Joan of Arc, Phidippides, Christopher Columbus, Nelson Mandela, William Blake, Pablo Picasso, Frank Lloyd Wright, the Beatles, Leonardo da Vinci, Mount Everest, James Joyce, Wolfgang Amadeus Mozart, Barry John.

James Davy
(Auckland, New Zealand)

'You throw it and I'll catch it' is probably the most celebrated quotation in the history of Welsh rugby. Yet, it sums up Barry John's approach to the game – unpretentious, uncomplicated, calm, unruffled, but as with every top sportsman, his competitive drive was enormous. He was an athlete who flourished in the most intense of confrontations. He was the first rugby superstar and a possessor of that unquantifiable gift – vision.

Barry John encapsulated the modern rugby athlete. What set him apart from the rest of the players was his ability to assess a situation, to change a strategy and in general respond intuitively to feedback from the opposition and this at international level in the backyard of the formidable All Blacks in 1971. This is what separated Barry John from so many other fly-halves, the brilliant performer from the good one!

'The King' was never mechanical, and was always guided by instinct, and Carwyn (in 1971), for one, trusted his instinct and vision. He was no doubt an artist not an artisan. He made an impact on every rugby follower's emotions and inspired my devotion to be the No. 1 supporter in the BJ fan club.

Barry was an intellectual rugby athlete; he was always in command, composed, in control, always assessing the challenge and effecting the solution either by his boot or sleight of hand or ghosting through keyhole spaces. He brought an aesthetic presence and grace to a contest and always exhibited a sense of fun – even managing a smile! He defied orthodoxy and brought respectability to 'round the corner kicking'.

There's no glimmer of doubt in my mind that Barry retired at too young an age – an age when so many sportsmen blossom into greatness and become legendary figures. Barry John was touched by the Gods and had 'good style that in truth is that very character in a man's play which marks him off from the other men' (Neville Cardus).

Allan Lewis

Barry in Cardiff colours at Stradey Park.

ALAN JONES

He scored more than 36,000 first-class runs, reached a half-century every third game and a hundred every eleventh match, but he never won an England cap: he was presented with one after making one appearance against the Rest of the World in 1970, but the series was later downgraded.

Alan Jones still has the cap but not the title of a former England international. Were he playing now, he would be a fixture in a team woefully lacking batsmen with technique. Jones, a left-handed opener, reached 1,000 runs in a season 23 times, a feat bettered by only ten players and he made 36,049 runs, 34th in the all-time list: every player ahead of him was capped.

Had he played for a more fashionable county, perhaps he

The late Ray Fredericks (left) and Alan Jones opening the batting for Glamorgan at Swansea.

would have had the recognition he deserved, not just because he would have been watched more by the national selectors but because he would have played on better wickets.

Jones's batting average, 32.89, and his 56 centuries in 1,168 innings are relatively modest given the records of the leading county batsmen today, but he played in an era of uncovered wickets and, until the twilight of his career, he batted in a cap rather than a helmet. He would be formidably hard to remove on some of today's flat tracks and it is not fanciful to suggest that were he playing now, he would average around the 50 mark.

Jones played many memorable innings: an unbeaten 161 against West Indies at Swansea in 1966, an attack which included Wes Hall and Charlie Griffith, 99 against the 1968 Australians on the same ground, an unbeaten double century against Hampshire in Basingstoke in 1980, 187 against Somerset at Glastonbury in 1963 but arguably his best innings fell just short of the three-figure mark.

It summed up Alan Jones: his eye, his courage, his pugnacity, his ability to use a rock-like defence as a springboard for attack. It was against Lancashire in Cardiff in 1967, the first year of first-class cricket at Sophia Gardens with the Cardiff Arms Park ground being converted to rugby.

Glamorgan had been set 178 to win in little more than two hours in a rain-affected match. The light was appalling, the wicket was even worse and Lancashire had two of the quickest bowlers on the circuit in Ken Higgs and Ken Shuttleworth. Glamorgan collapsed in the gloom and Higgs and Shuttleworth smelled blood.

Jones held firm, a mixture of circumspection and aggression, and it was virtually dark when he hit the winning run to finish unbeaten on 95. The England selector Alec Bedser had been at the ground the previous day, but the rain drove him back to London. Had he remained, Jones's career may have taken a different direction. It was England's loss.

Paul Rees

BRYN JONES

Brynmor (Bryn) Jones became the most expensive player in Britain in 1938 when he joined Arsenal for the then record fee of £14,000 and became the sporting sensation of the year. From local football in Merthyr, he was given a trial at Southend and Swansea but was unsuccessful, and joined Glenavon in the Irish League. He returned to South Wales and played for Aberaman before he was seen by a Wolves scout and moved to the Midlands club for a fee of £1,500. He made his league debut in a few weeks, and his brilliant displays earned him impressive headlines in the press.

He was a splendid ball player, quick and elusive, with the ability to turn defences inside out. He created openings seemingly out of nothing with his long penetrating passes. He, however, lost some of his form while playing for Arsenal, and their manager George Allison thought a spell in the second team might help Bryn, but there was no respite from the publicity and 33,000 turned up to see him make his debut for the reserves.

He continued to play regularly when he served in the 34th Light AA Regiment in North Africa during the war, and later went on to play and coach at Norwich. He then ended his connection with the game and took on a newsagent business in Stoke Newington, London.

The Jones brothers of Merthyr had a huge success within the game in Wales with his brother Wil John playing for Merthyr who were then in the Football League. Another brother Ivor played for Swansea and West Bromwich Albion and was a close friend of Billy Meredith in the Welsh team. Ivor's son, Cliff Jones, won all possible honours in football when playing for Tottenham Hotspur in the 50s and 60s. Emlyn, the fourth brother, played for Everton and Southend. Bryn Jones died in 1958 at the age of 73 in Wood Green, London. He was one of the most talented Welsh footballers of the twentieth century.

Llyr Huws Gruffydd

CLIFF JONES

The facts are impressive. Fifty-nine caps for Wales and fifteen goals into the bargain, each a result of pace, courage, and perfect timing of the final shot or header. He won the First Division Championship and the FA Cup at Wembley – twice – with Tottenham, and was outside-left in the Spurs team that thrashed Atletico Madrid 5-1 to take the Cup Winners' Cup in 1963.

Useful credentials, but it's not the bare statistical bones that stand out when one thinks of Cliff Jones, one of the rich seam of Swansea talent that emerged during the 1950s. This was the wingers' winger. His first touch may not have been so sure, but once he had the ball under control he was off, darting and swerving down the left wing, the thrill of the run palpable, the crowd roaring their expectation. Up to the full-back, dip the right shoulder, push the ball past the defender with the outside of the left foot, and then the explosive acceleration outside his man and on to the by-line.

Cliff could run and run with the ball. I remember watching him in the black-and-white television pictures from Wembley in 1962, running and running to leave the right side of the Burnley defence in shreds as Tottenham won the Cup 3-1. I remember the raw excitement of his bursts many a time in the red shirt of his country at Ninian Park. There was the match against Scotland in 1964, and Wales losing 1-2 with five minutes remaining. Cliff picks up the ball on the right for once, and moves towards the defence, dips the left shoulder, pushes the ball outside them to the by-line, cuts it back to the middle and Ken Leek thunders in the equaliser. Cliff's inspiration had fired the whole team. Two minutes later Leek scored again and Wales were home and dry 3-2.

Cliff was also a permanent threat to any defence in the air. Nobody had a style quite like him, speeding in from the left wing like an Olympic sprinter for the electric but graceful leap to hang hawk-like in the air and meet the cross with a forceful header to the corner of the net. Such was the style of one of his most crucial goals, the one which beat England 2-1 at Cardiff in 1955.

Cliff Jones was a restless spirit, a swashbuckling raider sweeping down the wing on the high winds of adventure. Safe and sealed in the memory.

Robat Powel

Cliff Jones (left) with Ivor Allchurch.

CLIFF JONES

The bare facts of the career of William Clifford Jones make unexciting reading. The Llandovery College, Cambridge University, Cardiff and Wales fly-half played no more than thirteen times for his country between 1934 and 1938. He was most unlucky with injuries – he missed the whole of the 1936/37 season through a broken collar bone – and yet, in those pre-war years no one thrilled British crowds more than the brilliant, mercurial Jones.

He was the most darting, elusive and dazzling runner of his time, perhaps of all time, blessed with a dagger-like sidestep, speed off the mark and lightening acceleration which made him the darling of rugby fans. Jones himself never forgot the debt he owed to T. P. 'Pope' Williams, his coach at Llandovery College. In his book *Rugby Union* Jones wrote: 'For five winters I was privileged to learn rugby under his guidance and to profit by his experience, his kindly and shrewd criticisms and his indefatigable enthusiasm. Any success in the rugby world which has come my way is almost entirely due to the interest and skill of my guide, philosopher and friend.'

For hour after hour, regardless of rain and mud, sleet and snow, Williams, like a ring master, would make Jones run and handle and pass so that by the time he left Llandovery he had mastered all the arts of the fly-half. The balance, dexterity, acceleration and confidence that were the result of Pope's master classes made him the glamour boy of the 30s.

Against Scotland in 1934, his mid-field thrusts, sidestepping and swerving through the defence, were astonishing, and then in 1936, again at Murrayfield, Jones ran himself to a standstill, setting up attacks first before scoring a brilliant try himself, beating man after man in a dazzling long run. Against England in 1938 he spread dismay in the opposition ranks and it was a sad day when he suffered another bad injury when playing for Cardiff in what turned out to be his last game, at the start of the 1939 season, two days before the outbreak of World War II.

In the post-war years, Cliff Morgan, David Watkins, Barry John and Phil Bennett were to become world-rated stars, but for many, Cliff Jones remains to this day the most brilliant attacker in the history of Welsh rugby.

Huw S. Thomas

COLIN JONES

Colin Jones will be remembered forever as Wales's uncrowned champion of the world. Twice within five months the former Gorseinon gravedigger thought he had taken the supreme crown from Milton McCrory in America. Each time he suffered the heartbreak of not getting the decision.

When they first met for the WBC title in the rarefied atmosphere of Renok, Nevada in March 1983, the judges could not separate them after 12 gruelling rounds. It was a classic duel of wits – the Welshman's awesome punching power versus the stylish but less destructive McCrory – the bludgeon against the rapier.

Trailing in the early rounds, Jones staged a rousing comeback in what must go down as one of the most glorious world title scraps in fighting history. The draw meant that McCrory keept the coveted belt, though Colin was sure he had done enough to deserve the verdict, and one of the judges made him the winner by two rounds. So did his manager, the late Eddie Tomas, who had guided featherweight Howard Winstone and lightweight Ken Buchanan to world titles.

'McCrory won the early rounds, then Colin took over,' he said after the fight. 'He threw the crisper shots. They were worth six of McCrory's. Most of his were powderpuff punches. Had the fight been 15 rounds instead of 12, Colin would certainly be champion.'

Midway through the contest, Jones rocked his taller rival back on his heels with swinging blows that would have rendered him senseless had they been a fraction more accurate. The 'Iceman' looked ready to melt in the ninth – the round in which Jones had twice pulled out devastating punches to dispose of the classy Kirkland Laing in each of their British title battles. A terrific left staggered the American but he survived the round, and stayed out of further trouble for the rest of the fight by adopting a back pedalling strategy which was booed even by his own fans.

Having already emulated his mentor Thomas by winning British, Commonwealth and European titles, Jones was desperate for another chance to become Wales's fourth world champion after Jimmy Wilde, Freddy Welsh and Howard Winstone. The re-match took place in sweltering heat at the Dunes Hotel, Las Vegas in August 1983. Once more the fight ended in controversy, McCrory kept his crown on a split decision. Again Colin was just one punch away from glory. The bell rescued McCrory in the seventh as he reeled from a combination of brutal blows.

'I feel I should be talking as the champion,' a devastated Jones said at the press conference which followed the fight. 'I did a better job than in the first fight. He was on a survival run from the seventh.'

Protesting, Eddie Thomas said, 'Colin won more convincingly than in the first fight but he still didn't get the decision. There should have been a European judge.'

Jones made a valiant third bid for the ultimate prize when he fought Don Curry for the WBA belt at Birmingham in 1985. It ended in tears in the fourth round with his nose being split open so badly by the Cobra's venomous punches that the referee had to call a halt.

Jones did not fight again. Persistent back problems brought an end to an outstanding career in which he was undefeated British champion from 1980 to 1982, undefeated Commonwealth champion from 1981 to 1984, and undefeated European champion from 1982 to 1983.

Pound for pound one of the all time heaviest punchers in British boxing, Colin won 26 of his 30 fights, 23 of them inside the distance. His other defeat was a sensational disqualification in Cardiff for a punch the referee ruled had been delivered after American Curtis Ramsey had hit the canvas.

Karl Woodward

D. K. JONES

Ken and I were sporting rivals from our early teens and from neighbouring Grammar Schools; he from Gwendraeth and I from Llanelli. We competed through the age groups as sprinters, with Ken winning the Welsh Schools Under-15 100 yards in 1956 in a remarkable time of 10.6 seconds. Later on, he took a more moderate view to training which meant that I was able to catch up.

As Under-15 schoolboy outside-halves, we faced each other in a local trial match and my 'B' team was hammered out of sight, and Ken went on to win his cap. At Senior Schools level, I grew slightly and eventually played in the centre outside Ken, and between us we had exciting moments at a time when schools rugby had a high profile. While still in school in 1960, we won the Welsh Snelling Sevens with Llanelli at Cardiff Arms Park. We created such an impression that J. B. G. Thomas of the *Western Mail* predicted that we would be Wales's stars of the future. Ken, as a centre, fulfilled that prediction far more than I, despite the fact that the laws and attitudes of the early 60s militated against open field runners.

Ken was a brilliant runner with footballing sense, innate pace, and a devastating side-step off his right foot. One of the greatest individual tries I have ever seen was scored by Ken against the star-studded Irish Wolfhounds at a packed Stradey Park. Picking up a loose kick on the right on our 10 yard line, he began side-stepping apparently through the whole of the opposing team to finish up under the posts to a crescendo of sound.

Ken had a notorious, if attractive, laid-back attitude to the game, which is exemplified by two stories in particular. In those days, there could be time to spare in the centre as the half-backs kicked up and down the touch-lines, and Ken had a remarkable eye. In one dour Llanelli match, while I fussed and fretted about the game, Ken sauntered over, 'Who's that girl sitting by your girlfriend in the back of the stand?'

At another match at Stradey, on a bitterly cold day, the ball was being dropped regularly. In a lull, a voice boomed out, 'For God's sake, Jones, get a ***** bucket'. Ken strolled towards the packed Grandstand, seemed to pick out the individual, and stuck up two fingers. The crowd collapsed in laughter.

In this pantheon of a book for great players, Ken may not be an obvious choice to the general public, but he would be a star in today's game.

Brian Davies

Ken Jones's fine individual try for the Lions against South Africa 1962.

ERIC JONES

The hands hardened by working in a granite quarry, the same hands that pulled him safely to the peaks of the world's highest mountains, today serve coffee and tea at his café in Tremadog. Among his credits are the solo scaling of the north face of the Eiger, and on many of his climbs all he had for company was a red dragon on his yellow helmet.

With an impressive list of climbs and a worldwide reputation thanks to award-winning films made in the 1970s and 1980s, the father of two is very proud of his roots and always ready to help friends. I called by the café once as I was preparing to leave for Tibet, and without hesitation he offered to lend me any equipment I might need. At the time I had only known him for a few months.

Once whilst climbing in the Patagonian Andes he spotted a volcano which had never been scaled before. After he and his companions reached the summit, they named it the Cerro Mimosa in memory of the pioneering Welshmen who ventured to South America on the sailing ship Mimosa in the last century.

A reserved person, he has never been one for the limelight, but in 1998 he came to the attention of millions after a spectacular base jump off the Angel Falls in Venezuela. (Imagine standing on the edge of Grib Goch and stepping forward into space.) After falling for twelve seconds he pulled the rip cord which opened the parachute to save him from the rocks below.

But despite his appetite for tough climbs and base jumps, he has never been one for taking unnecessary risks. On Everest in 1978 as Reinhold Messner and Peter Habbeler became the first to climb it without using supplementary oxygen, Eric stayed at the camp at 26,000 feet. He decided it was not worth the risk of losing whole fingers, or possibly more. Even the magical pull of the summit of that legendary peak, which has

drawn many to their deaths, and the chance to create history, failed to conquer his own common sense.

Today he is still planning further trips and expeditions and I suspect that neither his climbing shoes nor canopy will be collecting dust for some time to come.

Llion Iwan

JEFF JONES

Imagine the scenario! The West Indies were one down in the 1967/68 series against England. They had been stoned by the hostile home crowd on the final day of the final test and, by lunchtime, it appeared that winning was beyond them. Suddenly, England collapsed, and with time running out, an extremely anxious Jeff Jones was left to negotiate the final over.

He was the number eleven batsman, had always been the number eleven batsman whose ability to score runs had depended solely on the edge through slips for four.

He had to face Lance Gibbs, one of the world's greatest spin bowlers but, miraculously, Jeff survived as England drew the test and consequently won the series. As a result, Glamorgan's greatest ever left-arm fast bowler is often remembered at Test level for this one over with the bat in his hand in the intimidating atmosphere of Georgetown, Guyana.

From his early days, Jeff Jones was mad keen on cricket. It was his teacher at Stebonheath School, Llanelli, Raymond Thomas who encouraged him to join Dafen Cricket Club and by the time he was thirteen the enthusiastic and dedicated cricketer was selected for the village first team. Before long he came to the notice of Glamorgan and in 1960, the eighteen year old graduated into the county's first team. In 1963/64 he toured India with England and played his first test match at Bombay, thus winning his first test cap before gaining his county cap. Previously, this feat had only been achieved by four other players.

During his short career Jeff Jones took 408 first-class wickets but his most remarkable season for Glamorgan was the summer of 1965 that included his best ever figures of 8-11 against Leicestershire on a lively wicket. At the end of that season he was selected to tour Australia and New Zealand with the MCC, the ultimate achievement for any British cricketer.

On that tour he recorded his best ever test figures of 6-118 in the Adelaide Test. He was at his very best on the hard overseas surfaces and his test record confirms this. Out of fifteen tests played, Jeff only represented England twice on home soil.

He possessed a long-strided approach and his short balls were bowled at such an angle that batsmen had great difficulty in avoiding them. He was, at times, simply lethal. He regarded Australia's Bill Lawry and Bobby Simpson as two of the most difficult batsmen he ever encountered. They were truly great players because, according to the Dafen express, they could create time for themselves – a precious commodity in any sportsperson.

He toured Pakistan with England in 1968, but only played in one match, returning home immediately with a serious elbow injury that had troubled and plagued him throughout the previous summer. Jeff had been unlucky with injuries during his career and this latest setback brought the curtain down on his first-class cricketing days. There is no doubt whatsover that he would have been a cricketing legend had he been able to carry on for another ten years.

According to Jeff, who could bowl at ninety miles per hour, his son Simon is even faster than the old man himself. Simon has already represented Glamorgan and his father believes that the younger model has the talent to go all the way.

Mansel Thomas

JONATHAN JONES

It was once said of rugby players, 'You won't know how you've played till you read John Reason's report in *The Sunday Telegraph* and then it's bound to have been badly!'

Four times Powerboat World Champion, Jonathan Jones, could instantly assess his performance. He did not have to wait for *The Sunday Telegraph*. More often than not he crossed the finishing line in front of the remainder of the field and was, according to the sport's aficionados, the embodiment of a true champion.

In the intimidating atmosphere of powerboat racing, Jonathan Jones has been a power in the land. Amidst the unrelenting cacophony of high-pitched noises, he has been able to coax and cajole his boat through to the front in the face of stern opposition.

With immaculate timing, the bank official from Cardigan ghosts through on the inside, weaves intricate patterns when boxed in, glides away majestically on the outside to frustrate the opposition. On occasions the boat rises up sharply like a Courtly Ambrose bouncer and then lunges away like a torpedo.

All his life Jonathan Jones wanted to race. Unfortunately, due to a lack of sponsors he has been unable to do so of late. In Wales we hail heroic losers. We seem unable to honour true champions. Vast amounts of money are always available to some. It seems that the world champion's innate spirit of adventure and breathtaking performances will just be cameos from the past.

Brychan Llyr

KEN JONES

Tredegar Iron Works. What images are conjured up here – industrial south Wales, thick plumes of smoke? Or is this the place in Virginia which supplied munitions to Robert E. Lee's army in the American Civil War? Ken Jones. Is this D. Ken Jones, he of the twinkling feet; Oxford Blue and Lion in 1962 and 1966? No; let us move east and return to an earlier era. Splendid athlete – sprinter and long jumper for Wales, silver medallist in the British relay team in the London Olympic Games in 1948, and European and Empire Games competitor. This is Ken Jones, one of the great exponents of wing play for Newport, Wales and the British Lions. Born a few years after the end of the Great War, he came into prominence on the cinder tracks and playing fields in the late 1940s, and continued to dazzle the spectator until the mid 50s.

Ken made his debut for the Welsh XV a short time before I was born. By the time I was old enough to appreciate the nuances of wing play – being in the correct position to collect a pass and hare for the try-line, confounding opponents and delighting onlookers with a surge of speed too great to halt – Ken had disappeared from the sporting stage.

Although the images are extremely vague, I do remember standing on the touch-line on Treherbert's rugby pitch one winter's day in the 1950s and watching Ken appearing for Newport in a charity match. Gaping incredulously at this famous sportsman strolling off the field at the end of play, I turned to my father and said, 'So, he is a famous rugby player, wow!'

Were Ken to appear on our television screens today, his famous try for Wales against New Zealand at Cardiff in 1953 would be repeated more times than Tony Blair's renowned pauses acted in the style of Hugh Grant. The score stood at 8 points apiece. Clem Thomas found himself near the left touchline and in possession of the ball and with what seemed great intelligence punted the ball diagonally towards the opposite touchline where it was gathered in by the sprinting Ken. In a few strides he was over the try-line and his action had broken the stalemate. Wales won. When asked years later how he had pinpointed the flying winger, Thomas declared that he had 'just hoofed the bloody ball across the field and there was Ken'.

Apart from the stunning try scored by Gareth Edwards for the Barbarians which signalled a game of high excitement and ultimately a marvellous victory over the All Blacks of 1973, New Zealand have not lost a game at Cardiff since falling to the Ken Jones try.

Today, Ken Jones would have an agent handling his affairs. He would be successfully produced, packaged, marketed and his image distributed via television and newspaper advertising, endorsing food, drink, razor blades, sports and fashion wear. This embodiment of Welsh manhood would be displayed with the sportsmen of the successful nations; the public school Englishman, the stony gazing South African, the haka-stanced New Zealander, and the debonair Frenchman.

His international record tells all: 44 caps and 17 tries for Wales in a decade. He was top try-scorer with 16 in 16 appearances for the 1950 British Lions on the New Zealand leg of their tour of the Antipodes. Two of these tries were scored against New Zealand in three tests. He was a great favourite of the crowds and in the New Zealand rugby almanack he was profiled as one of the five players of the year. It took until the 1970s before his record number of caps for his country was overtaken, and that by one of the greatest players the world has witnessed – Gareth Edwards.

For a long period following his retirement, Ken Jones wrote a weekly column for *The Sunday Express*. This again was an achievement. Ken and Bleddyn Williams were, with the exception of Dai Gent, the only players given the licence to pen their thoughts in a newspaper. The majority of the current crop of former

players have ghosted columns in the press, or anodyne 'autobiographies' written with the aid of professional writers. It is to be regretted that Ken has not extended his writing to a memoir. Cliff Morgan, a contemporary, waited until 1996 before issuing an autobiography, while fellow black and amber David Watkins, albeit of a later vintage, had two books devoted to his playing days.

A few years ago, I squeezed through an exit at the National Stadium in Cardiff with Ken Jones and John Gwilliam in close attendance. The occasion was a Wales-England encounter, and, once again, Wales had produced a performance of startling mediocrity. Striking up a conversation we were soon discussing the events of the afternoon. Ken shook his head sombrely and declared that Wales lacked the basic skills, and, until these were addressed, the future of the game in Wales was consigned to failure and humiliation at the hands of the 'lesser' nations. Happily, Graham Henry, the new Welsh coach, recruited from his native New Zealand, has introduced a brand of rugby that is putting a smile back on the faces of the Welsh team and the supporters. But that is another story…

John Jenkins

LEWIS JONES

The year is 1948; the place is a classroom in Gowerton Grammar School. A fair-haired pupil with a faraway look in my English lesson! He had just put away his viola after playing in the school orchestra in assembly.

A roar had greeted the Headmaster's announcement of his selection to play full-back for the Welsh Secondary Schools against France at Cardiff Arms Park. (That same match was to mark my debut as a BBC commentator!)

Both the previous year's centres, Trevor Brewer and Roy Bish, were still available, so Lewis played in the final trial at full-back. Genius was not to be denied. 'There's our next Welsh full-back,' Eric Evans, WRU Secretary had said.

During the French match, B. L. Jones, as he appeared on the programme, stopped the 14-stone right wing, Lalande, with a try-saving tackle.

On leaving school, he walked into the Neath team, and scored 18 points in his first game. For some time he graced the field at Stradey in Llanelli colours. When he signed league forms for Leeds, the town of Llanelli went into collective mourning.

His league achievements matched his illumination of the union game for Devonport Services, Llanelli and Wales; when called up for the Lions in New Zealand he dazzled the Kiwis and was top scorer.

His contemporaries Bleddyn Williams, Jack Matthews, Malcolm Thomas (and Cliff Davies – remember Twickenham 1950?) named him as one of the most naturally gifted players ever; his subtle skill, change of pace and timing of his immaculate pass created space and unselfish chances for others. He kicked immense distances with either foot, and effortlessly accumulated match-winning points.

A quiet, cultured man, never flamboyant on or off the field.

Gilbert Bennett

LOUISE JONES

As the gales swept across Swansea Bay, Louise Jones was enjoying a day's 'rest' in her Port Talbot home. This was a day of recuperation after several days of hard training, which involves some three hours on the bike every day. And yet, on this day off, house-work was waiting, and as her husband, Phil is a self-employed plumber, there was no shortage of paperwork waiting for her attention either! Phil is also busily involved with promoting the stars of the future through his work with the British Cycling Federation's Development Programme, but today he'd gone on a 'club ride' with their five-year-old son, Michael on the tandem.

As if that weren't enough, Hayley their five-year-old daughter fancied a breath of fresh air. So off Louise went with Hayley on the trailer behind the bike – this on the day that Neath and Aberavon rugby clubs decided to cancel their Welsh Cup fixture as it was too wet and rough to mud-wrestle. Don't our rugby players have a hard life?!

At an age where most champions consider retiring, this ex-champion of the Commonwealth Games cycling track is still at it, facing the elements and clocking up the miles. After representing Britain in the Olympic Games at Seoul and Barcelona, Louise has now set her sights on the Sydney Olympics. No one can doubt the will to succeed and the determination of the woman who began her career in 1977 with the Ogmore Vale Wheelers when she was only fourteen years old. A smile breaks through the wind and rain on that dismal February day as she recalls her golden moment, winning Gold for Wales in the Auckland Commonwealth Games in 1990. Two days of showers had caused a delay, meaning that twenty-four long hours had passed between the semi-final and the final in the women's sprint. She lost her first race against Julie Spate of Australia, but after her long wait, Louise wasn't going to give in when she was so close to the fulfilment of her dream. Louise won the next two races, bringing the Gold to Wales for the first time.

Before the Games, Louise had had to face a weekly journey as far as Leicester for many months to get meaningful practice races. Many times she was stymied by rain, but seeing the glistening medal around her neck was proof that the effort was well worth it.

Louise Jones represented Britain in the World Championships every year between 1987 and 1992, and amongst her many successes are gold medals for her unbroken victories in the Women's Sprint event in the British Track Racing Championships between 1986 and 1991. She then turned her attention to road racing, but fell during the race in the Olympic Games in Barcelona. That led to a complete break from the sport to raise a

family. Eight years later, Louise Jones is back in the team colours of GS Strada, and determined to secure her place in the British team for Sydney.*

Credit is surely due to Louise for her determination and her perseverance over the years, in a country which is very much the poor relative as far as investment in training and development is concerned. Having said that, if anyone dares cross Louise in a competitive mood, the air is said to turn blue!

If you happen to be driving in the Port Talbot area and see someone on a bike demanding more than their fair share of the road, I'll bet my bottom dollar that Louise will win every time! Beware the warning, and drive carefully!

* Louise didn't quite make it to Sydney in 2000 but don't bet against her pushing her bike to the starting line at Athens in 2004.

Wyn Gruffudd

PERCY JONES

Ask the casual sports fan to identify Wales's first world boxing champion and the chances are you will get the reply, 'Jimmy Wilde'. But before the Tylorstown Terror came a young man from nearby Porth: Percy Jones.

Born, appropriately, on Boxing Day in 1892, he learned his trade at the local miners' hall, working his way through the ranks to earn a shot at Cockney Bill Ladbury in January 1914 at London's posh National Sporting Club, the aristocratic home of the sport. At stake was the British flyweight title – but also the world championship, recently introduced for the eight-stone class, and recognised only in Europe.

Jones's 20-round points victory earned him both honours and he soon became a triple champion, adding the European crown with victory over the only man to have beaten him, Frenchman Eugene Criqui. But Percy was a growing boy and suffered tremendously in his attempt to make the weight for a defence

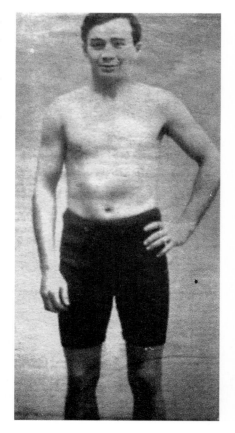

against Plymouth's Joe Symonds, who knocked him out in 18 rounds. The Jones reign had lasted just four months.

Within a year, Percy was involved in a bigger fight. He became a sergeant in the Rhondda Bantam Battalion, serving in France in that war which cost so many young lives. Old rival Ladbury was one boxer killed in action, while Jones was never to enter the ring again.

He returned to Wales a sick man, the effects of poison gas and trench fever taking their toll. He underwent no fewer than thirty operations, including the amputation of a leg, leaving him so weak that he had to be ferried around in a wheelchair.

When he attended a charity show at the Cardiff Empire in 1922, he weighed barely four stone, but still retained his sense of humour, telling Jim Driscoll: 'If you're short of an exhibition bout, I'll take you on.' He did not see the year out, dying on Christmas Day, the eve of his thirtieth birthday.

Gareth Jones

ROBERT JONES

'In the Beginning . . .'

No, there is no record that a huge bright comet streaked across the sky that night, and I can't recall that a fierce storm raged with incessant rain accompanied by thunder and lightning during that night of November 9th 1965. Not even Nostradamus himself had prophesised the birth of a remarkable baby on the following morning, November 10th.

But yes, a baby boy was born on that day in Cwm Tawe, a certain Robert Nicholas Jones – a second son to Cliff and Marian, and a baby brother to Anthony. The latest member of the Jones clan in Swansea Road, Trebanos.

In 1969, Robert placed his foot on the bottom rung of his educational ladder, and entered the village primary school, where Anthony was already a pupil and I was a teacher in the Juniors.

When I first cast eyes upon him, I was convinced a family of Chinese origin had moved into the valley, as both his eyes appeared partly closed as if seeking protection from some fierce glare of the sun or something! And I can assure you that he was not, as his middle name suggests, a saint. I had to remind him and his friend Mark Edwards on several occasions that the corridor was not the place to practice the 100 yard sprint.

By the time Robert had arrived in the juniors in the early 70s, it was patently obvious to everyone that he possessed extraordinary talents in all physical education activities, and his handling skills in rugby, cricket, soccer or rounders

were a joy to watch. Being so athletically co-ordinated and possessing good bodily balance made him an ideal folk dancer, especially when he was spinning or promenading Andrea (or was it Tanya, her twin sister?).

Such was the respect of the 'big' boys of the top classes towards Robert that they allowed him, a mere 8 or 9 year old, to join in their yard games. It was a pleasure to be on yard duty in those days, just to see him selling dummies, side-stepping and generally mesmerising the older boys with his audacious tricks.

In the formal games lessons, I had to ensure that both teams were evenly matched, which meant that 'Sir' would have to play on the opposite side to Robert. By the end of 40 minutes, on the yard remember, I would be red in the face, perspiring profusely and panting like a sheepdog after attempting to curtail his try-scoring demonstrations. Yes, the writing was well and truly on the wall as early as those days. And what thrilling and brilliant days they were too.

Eifion Price

In January 1999 I was present at a function in Stratford-upon-Avon listening to Dean Richards giving a speech. He was talking about the successful Lions tour of 1989. He described the changing room after their defeat in the First Test and how the smallest guy in the room spoke and inspired the team to succeed in the other Test Matches. Needless to say, the inspiration was Robert Jones, a man who has earned respect from fellow rugby players all over the world, as a player and as a man.

Robert and I go back to the late 70s when he started at Cwmtawe Comprehensive School, Pontardawe. He had been mentioned to me by Eifion

Price, his teacher at Trebannws Primary School, but my PE colleagues at Cwmtawe – Gwynne Lewis and Gethin Edwards – always spoke highly of his all-round ability in sport, not only as a rugby player.

When he was in the second year he was the captain of the team that won the Roehampton Sevens. I mention this because some things stick in your mind. Gwynne and Geth were in charge and we got through to the final – our opponents were Dulwich College. They had a super team and one star in particular; he was about twice the size of Robert and he had to carry his birth certificate around with him in order to prove his age. This match was I believe, Robert's entry onto the 'big' stage, a match that had attracted a lot of attention and support for both teams, and that was billed as a mini Wales v. England match. I can picture it now, the first time for a comprehensive school to get to the final and play just down the road from Twickenham.

The Dulwich pupil, a man amongst boys, broke through in the final and was about ten yards short of the try-line when Robert came from behind and put in a try-saving tackle which encouraged his team-mates to go and win! Six years after this match Robert was making his debut at Twickenham.

When he was a young boy his love for rugby football came through strongly and we, the PE staff, knew that he was destined for stardom. He was quick, very skilful, had the ability to make time for himself under pressure and he was brave both in the contact area and at exploiting space. Since those days, his record speaks for itself – from Welsh Schools to Wales, British Lions, Barbarians, *et al* – and the young man from Trebannws has achieved greatness in the game.

Wherever he has played he always gave his best, in successes and failures. Who can forget his performances for the Lions in Australia 1989 and his courage and skill when on the receiving end of a hiding from New Zealand in the World Cup 1987. From his schooldays onwards I watched Robert's progress through its 'highs' and 'lows' and he has always remained loyal to his roots in the Swansea Valley; he has always been a good role model for young players. Throughout his career Robert had a professional attitude towards the game both on and off the field, which could stand as a good example for the present professional players. Robert has earned the right to be up there with the giants of the game.

Geoff Davies

STEVE JONES

Athletes are a funny lot. Soccer and rugby players talk about being committed and training hard, but they don't know the half of it, at least not unless they have been on the road at 6am, training again at lunchtime, then back again in the evening. And that's training that hurts.

It is also why athletes usually look gaunt, drawn, or even ill, and there was no better example of that than Steve Jones, one of the greatest athletes Wales has produced. Jones took no prisoners. He was a pleasant, modest man and still is, but once that gun went he became an animal. All his aggression surfaced, he glazed over and settled into that ruthless, relentless rhythm that demoralised opponent after opponent.

They would try to hang on to him, as Charlie Spedding memorably did in the classic 1985 London Marathon. Spedding was himself at the top of world class, but Jones could drive himself into areas others could not. Towards the end the Newport man dug deep again and broke away to set a course record which still stands. Today he is living in Boulder, Colorado, enjoying permanent altitude training and still running every day. Needless to say he is still winning races.

He relaxes just a little more now, however. A couple of years ago he was asked to pace a group round the Chicago Marathon in three hours; chickenfeed to a sub 2:08 man like Jones, but very respectable for many club athletes. Jonesey thought he would look in at a blues bar the night before and found he liked the beer and the music. He stayed there all night, then got a lift to the race and jogged round in just under three hours. What happened next is unclear, but chances are he went back to the blues bar! Quite a guy.

Martin Pitchwell

FRED KEENOR

The renowned American inventor Thomas Alva Edison claimed, 'Genius is one per cent inspiration and ninety-nine per cent perspiration,' but the percentages would have to be adjusted in Fred Keenor's case. As Keenor's Cardiff City and Wales teammate Ernie Curtis said: 'Fred Keenor never gave up. The worse it got the harder and better he played. As a captain, he could somehow inspire the whole team.'

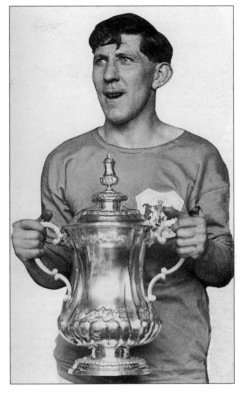

Keenor did precisely that when he led Cardiff to victory over Arsenal in the 1927 FA Cup final at Wembley and kept his word by doing so. Two years earlier Cardiff had lost in the final against Sheffield United and Keenor had vowed they would be back to make amends for that failure.

Cardiff also came within a whisker of winning the old First Division Championship under his leadership in 1924, so it was hardly surprising that the Ninian Park faithful chose Keenor as the club's biggest hero from any period in the Nationwide League's 'Local Heroes' opinion poll two years ago.

He was quite a hero for Wales too. With Keenor as captain, Wales won the Home International Championship in 1924, and he was nearly forty when he gained the last of his thirty-two caps in Scotland in 1933. According to Keenor after that game, 'I was so tired that I almost had to crawl off the pitch to the dressing-room.'

Not that Keenor was complaining – it wasn't in his nature. After he retired from football and despite the fact he was a diabetic, he worked as a labourer, getting up at half past four in the morning and walking five miles to the building site. You could argue that 'inspirational' is an adjective used too often when praising football captains nowadays but it's surely the best adjective to sum up Keenor.

Gareth Blainey

JACK KELSEY

Jack Kelsey had been a hero of mine ever since he joined Arsenal in 1951, eventually succeeding George Swindin as the Gunners' first choice goalkeeper. But it was in that match against Brazil on June 19, 1958 in the quarter finals of the World Cup that he became, to me, almost superhuman.

I well remember listening to the match broadcast live on our old Cossor radio with its dry and wet batteries, its dodgy connections making it sound as if someone was frying bacon down the line. I cheered when he saved from Didi. I cheered when he saved from Garrincha. I cheered when he saved from Santos. I cried when Pele scored the only goal of the match with a little over a quarter of an hour to go. Yes, I cried for Wales, I cried for myself. But most of all I cried for Jack Kelsey.

Jack at the time was bracketed with Lev Yashin and Harry Gregg as one of the three best keepers in the world. And the journalists who attended the World Cup competition in Sweden voted him the best keeper of the tournament.

It would be another twenty years before I was to meet my hero in person. I took my son, who was only four at the time, up to Highbury. And before kick-off I took him to the Arsenal shop where Jack was the manager. There was no mistaking him. The ex-blacksmith from Winch Wen stood behind the counter like a colossus. The diagonal scar across his face, suffered when he was twelve, was evident.

I bought my son an Arsenal shirt, ensuring that by doing so I would get to talk to Jack. As I wrote out my cheque he casually asked me where I was from. When

I told him I was from Aberystwyth he threw my cheque on the counter to make sure it didn't bounce. Then he held it up to the light.

'You never can tell with you bloody Cardis,' he quipped.

From that day I would never attend a match at Highbury without calling to see Jack. He was always humorous, always friendly. Always cracking jokes at the expense of us Cardis. I once asked him how he became such a good catcher of the ball. He told me that before a game he would take the chewing gum from his mouth and rub it on the palms of his hands. I laughed. It was only after his death in 1992 that I learned, that, for once, Jack hadn't been joking.

Lyn Ebenezer

TONY LEWIS

Tony is a year or two older than me, so I was a mere nipper when I read, enviously, of his debut for Glamorgan at the age of sixteen, when he still had two years to go at Neath Grammar School. This was an early indication of his great talent. We first met when we were opponents in the 1959 University Match, during which we had a few beers, as we have continued to do since.

Oxford won that game, and would have won in 1960, too, but for some interference from the weather and, more importantly, a notably resolute and technically excellent unbeaten ninety-odd from Tony as they held us off during the last two sessions.

In later years our paths continued to cross on the cricket field. When Glamorgan won the Championship in 1969 under Tony's captaincy I was playing for Gloucestershire. We were at the top of the Championship table in late July when Glamorgan came to Cheltenham, hammered us – I made 1 and 0 – and the Welsh county steamed on to take the title.

Tone was a shrewd captain, knowledgeable and inventive. He believed in a hard contest on the field but he also enjoyed a beer and a natter afterwards. The England party he took to India in 1972-3 was a happy one which came close to winning the series.

A lesser man than Lewis might have been prone to strut a little, for he got a rugby blue at Cambridge as well, and in addition to captaining England he has held down some pretty big jobs. He was for many years a highly respected broadcaster and journalist, former President of MCC and of Glamorgan, and Chairman of the Welsh Tourist Board. Through all this Tony has remained himself, affable, clever and funny; one of the good guys.

David Green

Fred (Trueman) never toured India with England. Tony Lewis did, as captain in 1972. He was a marvellously civil, genteel, humorous and much-loved leader. In India you have to be; they worship cricket. Five hundred autographs a day is the norm for a visiting net bowler. Lewis would sign his name into the night. One day, at Bangalore or Kanpur, or wherever, a man knocked on his door each hour of the day prior to the Test Match – 'My dear uncle, Lewis-sahib, please sign these sheets of paper for my big and beloved family!'

Tony would readily and dutifully sign each proffered piece 'A. R. Lewis'. By the second day of the Test, a gateman at last felt himself duty-bound to approach the England captain. Surely he had been too profligate with his invitations. Every sheet Tony had signed had been topped and tailed with the typewritten legend 'Please admit to Test Match. Signed, A. R. Lewis, Captain of England'.

Frank Keating

CARL LLEWELLYN

Ask any steeple-chasing jockey at the start of their careers if they could win one race, and I am sure that the majority would chose the Grand National at Aintree. The race, with its rich history and folklore is now famous on an international scale, and thousands of people flock to Liverpool each year to sample the excitement at first hand. It is the longest race, over four and a half miles in length. Courage, strength and agility are all required in both horse and jockey to conquer. But, luck has also played its fair share in the race.

In recent years, one of the luckiest jockeys must be Carl Llewellyn from Angle, in Pembrokeshire. He succeeded where jockeys such as Peter Scudamore

and John Francome failed; he raced to victory in the blue riband event of his sport and won the Grand National, not once, but twice within a decade. What's astonishing about both victories is the fact that he was not originally chosen to ride either of his winning mounts.

In 1992, General Election year, Party Politics, a giant of a horse trained by Nick Gaslee was amongst the favourites. After a number of promising runs, his regular partner Andrew Adams was looking forward to partnering him over Aintree's daunting fences. But unfortunately, fate dealt him a cruel blow, when he broke his leg in a fall some weeks prior to the big race. Carl Llewellyn was handed the responsibility, and gave Party Politics a dream ride to win the race for the first time.

Some might say that this was a chance in a lifetime, but history was about to repeat itself again and soon. In 1998, Earth Summit was a worthy favourite; he had won the Welsh Grand National earlier in the season, and the heavy going at Aintree was very much to his liking. Tom Jenks was his regular pilot, but unfortunately for him, as with Andrew Adams, he lost his golden opportunity by breaking his leg in a fall. Again, Llewellyn capitalised on the misfortunes of another and easily won the race aboard Earth Summit.

Now approaching his 37th birthday, time is not on his side to add to his victories in the race. But fortune and fate are definitely on his side, so you never know!

Wyn Jones

HARRY LLEWELLYN

Seconds to go. The horseman from Wales in his red coat walked his horse back and forth outside the huge show jumping arena. What was in his thoughts? How could he concentrate here in this competition, the pinnacle of his career? He faced the final round; the hopes and expectations of the other members of his team and, indeed, of a whole nation rested heavily on his shoulders. The first round of the competition had been a total nightmare for him with a total of 16.75 faults.

The two rounds had been pretty disappointing for the other two members of the British team, who had amassed between them a total of 24 faults. Things were not looking good. As he sat on his horse, he knew that this had to be a much improved performance – he had to put the uncertainties generated by the first round behind him.

He had to coax the big horse he rode; to reassure, to encourage – that's what he had to do. There was still a chance of glory; one round to go. Two fences down and all would be lost. Little wonder that he felt the burden of responsibility in every fibre of his body.

What had gone wrong in the first round? All the preparations had gone well – man and horse in perfect harmony; they understood each other completely. All those hours of work; they had reached peak fitness; they had successfully negotiated endless fences. A kaleidoscope of colours flashed before his eyes as he remembered.

He and the horse were a team. They had competed against the best and had beaten them. He had bought the well-bred horse five years ago as a six year old and they now had a telepathic understanding, each with total respect for the other.

What on earth had gone wrong? What if the recollections of the first round came back to haunt them once they were in the ring? And during the first round fiasco, he had almost fallen off!

The man on the horse forced all the doubts to the back of his mind. How, he didn't know. They walked into the ring. Somehow they succeeded in rediscovering the confidence and belief that had been the foundation of their partnership over the years. Man and horse believing in each other; the two in tune. The pain of the first round was expelled from their minds.

The horse had even dozed after that round, but now he was up on his toes, a coiled spring, eager to compete, to win. At the same moment, they both sensed that the readiness, the sharpness had returned – man and horse again in perfect harmony, each feeding off the confidence of the other.

While collecting themselves, while trotting gently into the ring to meet the challenge head on and to face the audience of thousands gathered around the ring, the horseman whispered, 'We have to concentrate, to time each jump perfectly'.

And away they go. Two moving in unison, eyes on each fence in turn, measuring each stride, looking for the perfect take-off point. The horse with ears

pricked, the horseman passing his instructions to him through his contact with the reins, checking and releasing, reassuring as the need arose. Their confidence growing from fence to fence. Flying over the last fence together to the deafening roar of the crowd. Overjoyed.

The place:	The Olympic Games in Helsinki 1952
The man:	Lieutenant Colonel Harry Llewellyn
The horse:	Foxhunter
The result:	Gold medal for the British team
	Harry Llewellyn – Foxhunter
	Wilf White – Nizefella
	Duggie Stewart – Aharlow (also from Harry's stable)
Their place in history:	Llewellyn and Foxhunter won a total of 78 International competitions including a bronze medal at the London Olympics in 1948.

Graham Williams

MATTHEW MAYNARD

Worcester, August 1997. Majestic swans on a slow flowing Severn, a blazing sun, the impressive cathedral shimmering in the haze, and 22 men engaged in a battle royal on New Road field. Wales versus England, but not a continuation of the border skirmishes prevalent in the area in days gone by, but a cricket match between Worcester and Glamorgan.

Both counties in mid-August had high hopes of becoming champions, and the Worcester batsmen were aware of this as they slowly amassed a total of 476 in the first innings. In reply, Glamorgan were a disappointing 155 for 6 before Mathew Maynard, with his familiar gait, reminiscent of a farmer walking his hills, strode to the wicket and proceeded to dispatch the ball to all corners of the ground during the next three hours. The timing had a poetic rhythm about it and the sound of bat on ball and ball against boundary fence was pure music, at least to Welsh ears. To some English ones as well.

According to Tom Graveney, this was the finest innings he had ever witnessed on the New Road ground. To be present was a privilege, to witness such an innings was to see a genius at work. Maynard the supreme artist, the magician weaving his magic spell over us. Words describing the experience are an inadequate substitute for being there to see such magnificence.

On the last day, Glamorgan needed 374 off 81 overs to win the match, and although the wickets started to tumble after a good start by Morris and James, no one was particularly worried. Maynard had still to make an appearance; Maynard the hero of the first innings. And then the moment arrived, as he came walking purposefully to the wicket before taking guard, looking around the ground and then settling down to receive the first ball from Haynes. And then, suddenly, it was all over; an edge to Rhodes the wicketkeeper, and the long walk to the pavilion with head bowed began. Glamorgan lost by 54 runs.

The match at Worcester was a microcosm of Maynard's career, of the ups and downs of his cricketing life. Supreme artistry one minute, unexplainable failure the next. But that is the nature of the genius, and the Welsh sporting public has forgiven every failure because it recognizes true talent and personality when it sees it. Not so the test selectors, who prefer the pedestrian colourless plodder to the eccentric genius.

A month later, the head that had been bowed on the last day at Worcester was held high in Taunton, as the man rejected by England but revered by Wales led Glamorgan to the county championship for the first time in 28 years. It was a champagne moment. There will be others, there will be colossal successes and staggering failures, because while Maynard continues to play the first-class game, cricket will never be dull and we can always expect the unexpected.

Elfyn Pritchard

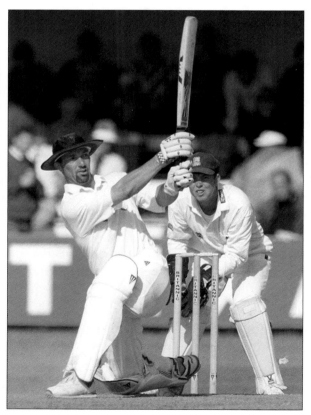

BILLY MEREDITH

Every genius on the sporting field possesses those heart-stopping skills, the technical perfection and the breathtaking ingenuity which always cause frenetic excitement among supporters. Billy Meredith was such an individual; the 'Welsh Wizard' was a legend in his own lifetime or, indeed, any other lifetime in a football context. An exceptionally fast and tricky winger, he was known as 'Old Skin' because his body, especially his legs, were so lean and bony. In his long, loose shorts, he would loiter menacingly out on the flank, expectantly waiting for his team-mates to supply him with constant possession. And when the ball duly arrived, he would pivot in whirligig fashion around defences on the right wing before delivering an inch-perfect pass or fire an

unstoppable shot at goal. He was a great favourite with the crowds, mainly because of the range of options available to him; his trickery flummoxed and perplexed defences. As a dribbler, he was way ahead of his time, and according to one commentator he resembled 'a slippery tadpole weaving its way through a pool of muddy water'.

Even during the 40s, when he regularly officiated at matches in the Manchester area, it was said that he used to dribble a ball around beer barrels in his cellar! With Billy Meredith, it was impossible to foresee what would happen next on the field of play. He was truly unique in his ability to execute back-heels to half-backs, and one of his favourite ploys was to change feet at the last instant before taking penalties. Cartoonists of the day revelled in depicting his eccentric custom of constantly chewing toothpicks throughout a match. They chanted from the terraces :

> *Oh! I wish I was you Billy Meredith*
> *I wish I was you, I envy you, indeed I do!*

He represented his country on every occasion with pride and passion. On 15 March 1920, a thick layer of snow covered Highbury when Meredith played his final match for Wales. He was 46 years old; at the time he was the oldest player ever to wear the Welsh shirt and no one since has achieved that distinction. Although he was first choice for Wales from 1895 to 1920, he had never been on a winning side against England. However, thanks to goals from Stan Davies and Dick Richards, the old enemy was defeated 2-1 and it was reported that Meredith wept openly in the changing rooms at the conclusion of play. Between 1894 and 1925, Meredith played in 1568 matches, scored 470 goals and won 48 international caps. He hung up his boots for the last time at the age of 50, and he remains a shining example to all sportsmen.

Geraint Jenkins

B. V. MEREDITH

To make a tour with the British Lions is the pinnacle of any rugby player's career, regardless of which era you belong to. Making three tours in seven years marks you out as a player of outstanding quality who earns his place in the folklore of the game. Brynley Victor Meredith is up there with the best.

It was no great coincidence that my career almost mirrored that of Bryn. As a sixth former in 1955, I had greatly admired his season in the Five Nations Championship and the part he played in the fantastic Lions side which toured South Africa at the end of the season. His achievements in the game are well documented, but it was the respect which the other players had for him which was so impressive.

As a captain, he was merciless and would stand no sloppy or irresponsible play. In my first major game for Newport against Leicester at Welford Road, I received the ball on the wing and cross-kicked, from which we scored, but in Bryn's eyes I had committed the cardinal sin of giving the opposition the opportunity to regain hard-won possession. I was told in no uncertain manner that I was not to repeat the action ever again.

Bryn Meredith (centre) captaining Wales 1960.

Conversely, when it came to playing against our great rivals, Cardiff, he was almost charitable. He had reached an unspoken arrangement with the Cardiff hookers that they would not strike for the ball against each other's put-in at the set scrum.

There was no doubt that he was a hard taskmaster and demanded that the players around him worked as hard and as uncomplainingly as he did. Very often, because of his intense pride in striking for the ball at the scrum, there was very little room for the second row to place his head and shoulders between him and the prop and it embarrasses me to say that often I had to scrummage with my head between his legs!

I have always thought that Bryn Meredith was the type of player and personality who would have suited and excelled in his position in any era. As a player and a leader he inspired all to reach the very high standards he set himself.

What typified his attitude to the game and to the ethos of team spirit was his reaction to the fact that although he was by far the best hooker on the 1959 Lions tour to New Zealand (he never played in the Tests because the tour captain was the Irish hooker, Ronnie Dawson) his enthusiasm never wavered. He gave his all, supporting his captain and colleagues at all times. Just what you would expect of such a great man!

Brian Price

JOHN MERRIMAN

In the summer of 1957, I was on a school trip with a group from Amman Valley Grammar School. It was a ten-day rail trip taking in Venice, Florence and Rome, with the first few days centred on a strictly run 'guest' convent, which was next door to the Venetian jail. The cost of the trip was £29/15s/0d and as luck would have it, a fifteen year 'penny policy' of life insurance matured in our house that year to the tune of £29/19s/6d, so my parents kindly agreed to blow it on me.

I really fancied the school trip of '58 as well, but no 'penny policy' was due to mature, so my one taste of adventure that year was a day at the British Empire and Commonwealth Games in Cardiff. Fate was kind to me that year. I found myself with friends in the North Stand at Cardiff Arms Park enjoying the athletic events.

Now, I have to say that over the years I have been privileged to watch many sportsmen grace that stadium who

would clearly qualify as Welsh sporting giants of the twentieth century. The list of rugby players alone would fill two double-decker buses, but on my '58 day at the Games it was a Welsh athlete who struck a match to fire a nation's enthusiasm and roaring support.

It was in the '6 mile' final that the grandstand seats became superfluous as we all stood and willed our man in the red vest to the finishing tape.

As the race progressed we had merely glanced at our programmes, but as the runners began to string out over lap after lap, we gradually noticed that a red vest was "hanging on in there". Not only was he hanging on, but he was fourth, then third, then second and then so close he could have picked the pocket of the Australian in front.

The Australian's name was Power and he was full of it, but our man was worrying him. Who was he anyway? Programmes began to flap. Where's he from? Who cares, he's Welsh isn't he? What's his name? John Merriman.

By the last lap we were all related to him. We roared him along the back straight, leant with him into the final turn and as he pulled out to make his effort on Power's shoulder, we all screamed 'NOW . . . take him NOW!' 'You've got him . . . YEEEEEEEES!!!!!!!!'

No. it wasn't to be. He did his best, but that fellow Power was a piston of locomotion. He got the gold, and our man Merriman got the silver.

I don't suppose he truly qualifies as a 'sporting giant', but what a 'giant of a sporting day' it was. For all the greats I've had the pleasure of seeing, that half hour in the 1958 British Empire and Commonwealth Games with John Merriman still brings a tingle in the memory.

Roy Noble

CLIFF MORGAN

Wales is a land where, according to the legend, there are outside-half factories dotted all over the place and if it is to be believed, Max Boyce, our own rugby troubadour is still on the trail of these elusive creative workshops. To every rugby loving Welshman, any player wearing the No. 10 jersey is a God – we treasure them and give them 'superstar status'. The list is endless, from Billie Trew, Cliff Jones, Willie Davies, Billy Cleaver, Dai Watkins, Barry John, Phil Bennett and Jonathan Davies through to today's superstars Neil Jenkins, Arwel Thomas and the latest icon, Iestyn Harris.

There have always been great debates about who is the greatest outside-half of all time. Everyone has his or her own opinion. Cliff Morgan played twenty-nine times in the red jersey of Wales in an international career spanning eight years. He was the most capped fly-half of all time before being emulated by Phil Bennett in the golden era in the 70s and most recently overtaken by Neil Jenkins. In Cliff's days, caps were hard to come by and were usually gained during the Five Nations Championship.

A man of the Rhondda, Clifford Isaac Morgan graced the Welsh rugby season during the 50s and immortalised himself on the British Lions tour of South Africa in 1955, scoring a memorable try in the historic 23-22 win in the First Test.

A pocket dynamo, he was only 5ft 7 ins in his bare socks, but he had a brave heart and thought nothing of falling on the ball – he had searing acceleration and, like so many great Welsh fly-halves, he could win a game on his own. Cliff did become a rugby and broadcasting legend, but in his greatness he had a touch of humility. He was a man who never courted success, who had a great affinity with the game and the people who make up the rugby fraternity. Despite spending the greater part of his professional life working in London in the higher echelons of the BBC, he never forgot his background and his Welshness.

To be in the presence of Cliff Morgan you know that he is of that rare vintage, of the same mould as his great contemporary, the late and great Carwyn James. They were knowledgeable individuals, both capable of keeping you spellbound, men of rugby intellect.

Cliff Morgan's contribution to Welsh rugby is simply immense, as a player and commentator. Who can forget his immortal words when Gareth Edwards scored one of the greatest tries of all time for the Barbarians v. New Zealand at Cardiff Arms Park in 1973, one of the truly great moments of international sport, a try started by Phil Bennett under the shadow of his own posts and ended with Gareth's spectacular dive in the corner at the Taff End, 'It's out to Edwards – he's going to score – Oh! what a try – brilliant!'

Royston James

DAVID MORGAN

David Morgan, the Welsh weight-lifter, has won more Commonwealth gold medals than any other Welshman. He began his career in the 1982 Commonwealth Games at Brisbane, Australia, the scene of a thrilling battle for the gold in the 67.5 kg class.

David was only 18 years and 2 days old, and hardly anyone believed he had the faintest chance of winning any medal. He had two experienced coaches in his corner, Den Welch and Myrddin John, and the day began well for David as he weighed in at 67.05 kg, the lightest of the 8 contestants, providing him with an important tactical advantage.

The hotly tipped favourite was Australian Bill Stellios, but the home crowd was in for a shock when they saw David equal Bill's first attempt at 120 Kg, and then immediately ask for 127.5 Kg. Stellios then asked for 125 and was successful at the first attempt. Wales called for 130 but David was disappointed as he failed to lift that weight. Stellios then had to attempt 130 Kg, as Patrick Bassey of Nigeria also finished at 127.5 Kg. He failed. David re-attempted that weigt and lifted it effortlessly. To the amazement of Stellios and the Australians, Wales then called for David to lift 140 Kg at his last lift. Stellios took to the stage for his final lift, but his heart wasn't in it, and, visibly strained, he failed miserably. As a result, the Wales team dropped back to a more realistic 132.5 Kg, and David yet again executed a perfect lift.

David was by now 7.5 Kg ahead of Stelios and 5 Kg ahead of Bassey, who made it to 150 Kg to secure the bronze. Stellios began with a 150 Kg lift, and David failed to follow at the first attempt, but made it at the second. At the third attempt, he went for 162.5, rather than 165, and succeeded again.

The Welsh team now had to sit back and wait, as Stellios had two attempts left. He asked for 172.5, the weight he would need to secure gold, as he was heavier than David. Although he managed to lift the bar as far as his shoulders, his attempt to raise and hold the bar above his head failed, not once, but twice, and after a nail-biting finish, the Welshman was victorious!

David went on to win another gold in 1986, three golds in 1990, two golds and a silver in 1994 and a silver in 1998.

Delyth Mainwaring

HYWEL MORGAN

Hywel Morgan, born into the household of Moc Morgan at Pontrhydfendigaid, was destined to have a profound interest in fishing. He often explains that, unlike other babies who are given a rattle of some description to amuse themselves, he was given a fishing reel. He grew fond of its music at a very tender age!

However, although he began fishing at the age of three, Hywel only began taking the sport of casting very seriously in his early teens. Casting, while akin to the sport of fishing, demands a more professional approach.

Hywel was lucky in that he was taken to Jack Martin, then the top caster in the UK, and a six-time

winner of the World Champion Casting Tournament. Martin was a perfectionist and instilled in Hywel the importance of correct technique. Without this strict approach, Hywel would not have achieved the level of expertise and performance that he later attained.

At the age of thirteen, Hywel began competing in game fairs and casting competitions, but was soon debarred because of his success in collecting all the trophies. He then took an interest in international and world casting competitions. By the time he was sixteen, Hywel had established himself as the top caster in the UK, and still holds to this day fourteen British casting records. One record, that of distance casting, done with a single-handed rod, is the longest single-handed cast ever made in the world under international casting rules, measuring eighty metres, fifty-four centimetres. It is extremely unlikely that that particular distance cast will ever be bettered.

At sixteen years of age, Hywel had his first attempt in European casting tournaments in Paris and won gold for the distance competition. He then went to Canada, still at the age of sixteen, to cast in the World Casting Championship. He was the only competitor from Britain in the tournament. Therefore, he was captain, manager, baggage man, and carried the Union Jack – in short, he was the complete British team, and he took fourth position in the distance casting event. At the Senior World Championship in Canada, he missed the medals by only a few centimetres!

Hywel made Europe his happy hunting ground for medals and trophies. In 1987, he won the European Championship in Berlin for distance casting. In the World Games in Holland in 1993, he won the accuracy competition. He also managed a silver in the distance event in the World Games in London. There, Hywel was very surprised to learn that the Czechs had made a video of him perfecting the distance casting event, and it made him realise that his style of distance casting was becoming very popular. One member of the Czech team, as they stood on the podium to receive their medals, asked Hywel: 'Will the Queen now be coming to your house to congratulate you?' Yes, some countries take the sport of casting very seriously and honour their successful sportsmen.

Recently, Hywel has taken up casting with multiple rods. In the TV programme *Record Breakers*, which was recorded in Rome, he cast with no less than 66 rods simultaneously (thirty-three rods in each hand). This is the present World Record in Multiple Rod casting.

Eilir Owen

KELLY MORGAN

A young Welshwoman and a true product of her area and country, Kelly Morgan is often to be seen celebrating a victory at the end of some foreign competition sporting a Welsh flag. Grace of movement and speed on the badminton court are also Kelly's trademarks.

While during her childhood Kelly was interested in various forms of dance, including tap, modern and ballet, she soon became interested in sport, an integral part of the culture of the Pontypridd area. It was whilst watching a game of badminton involving friends and members of her family that Kelly's love of the sport was sparked. A year later, a ten-year-old Kelly took part in the Welsh trials. Despite losing every game, the young girl had succeeded in drawing the trainers' attention. Kelly's sporting abilities developed gradually during her formative teenage years. However, her play remained undistinguished; a fact which resulted in her trainer demanding further commitment in order that Kelly make it to the top of her sporting profession.

Deciding to specialise in badminton, Kelly's ability in this skilled sport blossomed. And as she spent two years as one of the practising partners in the Olympic team's centre in France, Kelly's talent was both nurtured and given direction. This instructive period was followed by a year in Denmark, where Kelly played for the Højbjerg club before going on to join the German club, Regensburg.

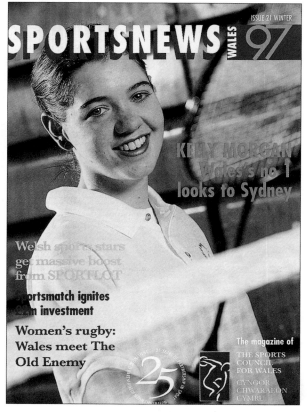

Soon Kelly Morgan was the British female champion. A silver medal in the European championships was followed by gold at the end of the 1998 Kuala Lumpur games – a phenomenal achievement considering that some of the world's foremost players were competing.

In Copenhagen, Kelly was again seen beating the world's best including Ye Zhaoying from China. Although she failed to go on and win this particular championship, her performance proved her worthy to take her place alongside the other world-ranked badminton players.

Ion Thomas

HUGH MORRIS

The script could not have been better. Fate, or rather a tasty job offer from the ECB, decreed that Hugh Morris's last match for Glamorgan would be the championship clincher in 1997 – an opportunity for his beloved county to win the pennant after a period of 28 years. Just for good measure, he scored 165 to equal Alan Jones's club record of 52 centuries. He could, and maybe should, have scored the winning runs in the second innings, but yours truly somehow managed that amidst the mayhem and celebration.

Hugh's retirement came as an enormous surprise to us all. In fact, most of us only got to hear anything of it on the second evening of that historic match. After our daily end of play soccer kickaround, he called us all together to warn us because the press had got wind of the fact that he was in line to replace Micky Stewart as Technical Director at the ECB. Despite constant knee problems throughout his career, 1997 had seen him at his fittest for a long while and surely he had many years left in him.

I was stunned because I was at last beginning to contribute something to an opening partnership which was flourishing after initial spluttering due to my technical deficiencies and inconsistency. He was the ideal partner in all respects, and the biggest compliment I can pay him is to say that I was always surprised when he was out. To me he rarely looked in trouble, and I yearned for his calm and poise. Hugh had a voracious appetite for batting (as 19,785 first-class runs testify) which was almost matched by his desire for food. Somewhat surprisingly, his dressing room nickname was Banners, from the TV detective Banacek, rather than some gastronomical reference.

Hugh played only three Test matches for England, scant reward for being one of county cricket's most reliable opening batsmen of recent times. However, he did captain England A on three overseas tours and led his county in two separate stints, the first at the tender age of 23. He was skipper at Canterbury in 1993 on that famous day when Glamorgan lifted the AXA Equity & Law title – a popular victory for an extremely well-liked man who left the game with no one having a bad word to say about him – although there was that time when he dropped me!

Steve James

GILBERT PARKHOUSE

The very mention of Gilbert Parkhouse will, for many, evoke memories of an elegant right-handed batsman who opened for Glamorgan with great distinction for many seasons and always appeared to be fully at ease against the quickest and most hostile of fast bowlers in the world.

There were many of quality: Statham, Trueman, Tyson, Loader; Lindwall and Miller; Heine and Adcock; Hall and Griffith and many more. All were instantly judged on line and length and played accordingly from either front or back foot with perfect technique and wonderful timing.

Frequently, one wondered how one so slim could propel the ball through the covers at such a velocity. Gilbert was never intimidated by short-pitched deliveries and, more often than not, would accept the implied challenge by hooking or pulling with power. And this was before the age of protective helmets!

115

Faced by the certainty of having to play many matches on wet, slow or 'turning' pitches, he honed his skills to deal with many class spinners plying their cunning trade. Gilbert was one of the very few to 'read' the variations of the great 'Sonny' Ramadhin. The 'sweep' shot and the delicate late-cut became major sources of runs, and by the mid-50s, he was the complete batsman and regularly topped the Glamorgan run aggregate.

But for great contemporary opening batsmen – Len Hutton, Cyril Washbrook, Reg Simpson and others of 'high class', Parky would have gained more than seven caps and one major tour to Australia.

Most games came effortlessly. He was a fine rugby player for the 'All Whites', he played hockey for Wales and badminton to a high standard, but he excelled at cricket, as one would expect of a lad born within a six-hit of St. Helens and coached in his formative years by the legendary W. J. Bancroft of Swansea, Glamorgan and Wales fame.

Gilbert Parkhouse is, without doubt, one of the all-time Glamorgan greats and it was always a pleasure to play alongside him and watch him at the crease.

Don Shepherd

BERWYN PRICE

cantabrian

It's late afternoon in 1969, on a damp windswept Aberystwyth University Athletics track, high on Penglais Hill overlooking Cardigan Bay. A coaching session is underway. Gwyn Evans, the coach, is putting two high hurdlers through their paces. The senior athlete, Graham Gower, is currently the Great Britain No. 2 over the 110 metre hurdles; the second more junior athlete is a tall, lean and long-legged fresher by the name of Berwyn Price.

After completing their various drills and technique sessions, Gwyn Evans stood and watched as the enthusiastic young fresher snapped over the hurdles, his baggy track suit bottoms brushing each barrier as he hurdled each set. As they raced, the young fresher was pushing the senior athlete to greater endeavours in his efforts to keep ahead. 'Raw but quick' was the coach's initial assessment.

Born in Tredegar in 1951 and educated at Lewis School, Pengam, the gangly eighteen-year-old from the South Wales valleys was clearly a talent to be nurtured and cultivated. A training regime of weight training, sprint work, technique sessions, hurdling manoeuvres and fartlek drills over the sand dunes of Ynyslas soon bore fruit.

That first year at University in Aberystwyth proved to be a busy one for the young Berwyn Price. He quickly surpassed his contemporary, Graham Gower, by beating him at the Welsh University championships at Swansea. He rapidly moved on to greater achievements and in 1970, whilst still in his freshman year, he competed for Wales in the Commonwealth Games at Edinburgh and became European Junior 110 metre hurdles champion in Paris. In these days of full time professional athletes, it is worth noting that, while obtaining an honours degree in economics, Berwyn found time to represent Wales and Great Britain in European and Commonwealth Championships and in the Olympics at Montreal in 1976.

He subsequently ousted Alan Pascoe as the British No. 1 over 110 metre hurdles and was the British Champion for six consecutive seasons (1973 – 78). He held the Welsh, British and Commonwealth records and became the World Student Games Champion in Moscow in 1973.

His hour of glory was to come in Edmonton, Canada at the 1978 Commonwealth Games. As overall captain of the Welsh team, he led by example, winning the gold medal in his event. A much admired and respected athlete in world athletics, Berwyn went on to captain the Great Britain athletics team at the Montreal Olympics in 1976. He competed for Wales in four Commonwealth Games championships from 1970 to 1982. He graced three European championships from 1971 to 1978, and represented Great Britain on over 50 occasions at international meets.

His coach, Gwyn Evans, who was to die prematurely in 1988 at the age of 57, always thought that Berwyn's best event would ultimately prove to be the 400 metre hurdles. But Berwyn always rejected the idea of a serious move to the one lap event, claiming that he was a sprinter not an endurance athlete. However, his oft repeated claims to his coach that 'long runs kill me' have subsequently been proved wrong; Berwyn has completed both the 1994 and 1995 London Marathons – not bad for a sprinter!

Rhodri Evans

GRAHAM PRICE

Ask any fly-half to name a few of his favourite players and you would expect the names of Barry John, Phil Bennett and co. to trip off the tongue with consummate ease. This erstwhile fly-half is no exception, but high up on the list would also be the name of a tight-head prop – Graham Price.

He is the third, and Bobby and Tony must excuse me if I say also the most talented, of the world renowned Pontypool front row. This feared and highly respected triumvirate from the Gwent valleys reigned supreme as the cornerstone of the much vaunted Wales Grand Slam teams of the 1970s.

Graham Price, however, stood out as an outstanding footballer who could also 'mix it' with the toughest of them in that frenzied and mystical world of the front row brigade. On my first trip to Australia with Wales in 1978, I would often find myself at the end of training sessions practising my goal-kicking and drop-kicking at Ballymore or the Sydney Cricket Ground. One to continually throw out a challenge would be the quietly spoken tight-head prop who, but for his physique and strength, could surely have played fly-half or centre at the highest level.

I will not disclose the outcome of those kicking competitions. Suffice to say that I remember the gauntlet being thrown down and to stress that the kicking contests would have been far more competitive than if I had challenged Pricey to an arm wrestling competition.

I have two other images of Graham, apart from him being one of the game's great gentlemen. The first is that incredible run the whole length of the field that saw him score against France at the Parc des Princes in 1975. That was a marvellous moment and a tribute to his great fitness and skill in being able to run that distance at the end of a gruelling and physical match against a great French outfit.

The second was the sorry sight of Graham sitting on the British Airways flight coming home from Sydney on the ill-fated 1978 tour with his jaw held in place by the crudest of bandages. This injury resulted from a sneaky and cowardly punch by Australian barrister Steve Finnane that broke his jaw in the second test at Sydney.

Despite the hurt, I never heard Graham utter one word of complaint concerning the incident. He could look after himself, he could dish it out, and he could also take it! A great player and a magnificent individual. Oh! For a Graham Price in the modern game.

Gareth Davies

JOHN PRICE

True champions don't always succeed. It takes grit, determination, personality, perseverance and a certain amount of innate ability to get to the top. According to John Price the three key words are 'practice, practice and practice':

> *A concert pianist sits at the piano and runs his hands up and down the keys. Five hours a day, every day. Very repetitive. Then he goes along to the concert, sits down to play and he's perfect. Every time. That's what I'm after.*

However, the man who dominated the world of bowls in the 90s always remembers his introduction to the sport when he lost his very first tournament at Skewen near Neath in the first round. That proved a harsh lesson to the young twelve year old, a lesson he still remembers vividly.

John Price was born on the 14th of September 1960 to Harry and Margaret Price. He was educated at Glan-y-Môr Primary School and Sandfields Comprehensive School. He was a talented young footballer but was soon influenced by members of his family who were enthusiastic bowlers in the community. He was regularly to be seen practising with his father and two grandfathers on the immaculate Ynys greens at Port Talbot.

Upon leaving school at eighteen years of age, John joined the Civil Service and diligently spent twenty years in the Social Services. These days, John is involved in marketing with a well-known bowls manufacturer, constantly talking about and being involved with a game that is part and parcel of his lifestyle. John is a man of the people; the common touch has always prevailed and there is nothing he enjoys more than going along to his club at Ynys and playing with and against his friends, putting the tension of competitive championships to one side.

He became Singles Champion at Port Talbot at the tender age of fourteen; he represented his country for the first time in an international indoor event against Ireland five years later. Without question, one of the highlights in a memorable career is when he partnered his father Harri in a Pairs Tournament in 1982. Several great sportsmen and women have competed with or against their parents but how many can say that they won a major championship partnered by a mother or father?

John Price's name became synonymous with bowling excellence in the early 90s when he became World Indoor Bowls Champion. And with television promoting the sport, the bowler from the Afan Valley became something of a hero and a role model in the sport. There was a long list of successes, including; British Indoor Champion in 1993 and 1996.

John's current partner is Stephen Rees and the combination is proving particularly fluent and effective. Both seem to understand each other instinctively, and in 1999 won the World Pairs title. Medals were won at Victoria and Kuala Lumpur, and one of the most memorable matches was against Rowan Brassey of New Zealand. Price trailed 9-19 but the Welshman fought to the bitter end and eventually achieved an incredible victory. John Price – a true champion.

Mel Morgans

TOM MALDWYN PRYCE

A small country needs its heroes – brave souls who carve their homeland's name on the world map, inspire national pride and bring a sparkle to the lives of its citizens. And it naturally follows that the loss of such a hero will be keenly felt.

Cast very much in this mould was Tom Pryce, the greatest driver ever produced by Wales. And, although it is 24 years since his tragic death, Formula One Racing, despite all its glamour and excitement, has never been quite the same for his many fans.

Thomas Maldwyn Pryce was born on June 11, 1949, at Trevalyn Manor, Rossett, near Wrexham (then a maternity home). As his father John was a police officer, Tom and the family moved frequently – Brymbo, Denbigh, Tywyn, Abergele and eventually Ruthin, where Tom trained to be an agricultural engineer. In the Welsh-speaking household he was always known as Maldwyn.

Every aspiring Formula One driver needs inspiration, and Tom gained his from his father, a keen motor-racing fan, who took him to Oulton Park and Aintree where, in 1955, they saw the unforgettable occasion in the British Grand Prix of Moss and Fangio trouncing the opposition 1-2 in their Mercedes cars. Throughout Tom's racing career his father was his guide, mentor and, above all, friend.

Like many of today's top drivers, Tom started off by attending motor-racing schools, where his natural talent quickly showed through. He then followed the classic route to the top through Formula Ford, Formula Super Vee and eventually Formula 3, which gave him his first break. Well, two actually, and both at Monaco! In 1972 he was standing by his Royale which had broken down at the side of the track when another car lost control in the wet and ploughed into him, breaking his leg!

But in 1974 the break was of an altogether happier kind when he won the supporting race to the Grand Prix in fine style. The 'up and coming man' had arrived, and where better than the Mediterranean millionaires' playground before the world media and, more importantly, Formula 1 team managers. The offers came flooding in and Tom chose Shadow, managed by fellow Welshman Alan Rees of Monmouth.

In 1975 he had his best result, winning the non-title 'Race of Champions' at Brands Hatch, was fourth in the German Grand Prix and third in the Austrian. He also qualified in pole position for the British Grand Prix at Silverstone.

In the end, fate cruelly decreed that the young Welshman's talents would never have the chance to blossom with one of the top teams. In the South African Grand Prix at Kyalami on March 5, 1977, a young, inexperienced fire marshal ran across the track to attend a minor fire, ironically in team-mate Zorzi's Shadow. At that moment, Tom came blasting flat out over a slight brow at over 170 mph, and the resulting collision killed both the marshal and Tom himself, who was struck by the fire extinguisher. Motor-racing lost a courageous, unassuming character tipped by many to be a future World Champion, and Wales one of her finest ambassadors. Tom was a racer, pure and simple, not a quasi-businessman. As his father said, 'All he ever wanted to do was get his backside into a racing car.'

John. A. Edwards
Country Quest

MARILYN PUGH

Marilyn began her hockey at Ystalyfera and Cwmtawe School. She played for Glamorgan and South Wales before winning her first International Cap when she played in the first ever Welsh Schoolgirl Team in 1971.

There followed a wonderful international career. She played for the Welsh Under-23 Team before being awarded her first Senior Cap in 1973 when she played against Scotland at Llandarcy. From this time until her retirement in 1985 she was an ever-present member of the team – probably one of the first names on the team sheet. The only games I can recall her not playing were either through illness or injury. She was a very special player, undoubtedly the best right wing I ever played with and arguably, in her time, one of the best in the world. She was so very talented – fast, with very quick and neat footwork, skilful, dynamic, composed, compact – are just some of the words which describe her abilities. All her team-mates would concur that 'she was great to play with and that if we could get the ball to her we would create huge problems for the opposition.' Thus, in both training and in tactical talks, getting the ball to Marilyn became one of our major objectives. She scored lots of goals, she had great anticipation, and an uncanny knack of timing her runs to the goal and getting in on the end of crosses from the left. The call of 'with you' became synonymous with Marilyn.

Her composure in front of goal was amazing and in a one-versus-one situation, i.e. goalkeeper-versus-attacker, the odds would normally be 50/50, but if the attacker was Marilyn the odds would always be much greater in her favour. She never resorted to blasting the ball past the goalkeeper, but rather she used her wide variety of skills to put the ball in the net.

Wales's greatest achievement was in 1975 when we reached the final of the World Cup in Edinburgh. Marilyn played a significant part in that campaign, creating and scoring goals and causing a problem to opponents. It was at this tournament that her outstanding talents were seen and recognised by the rest of the world.

Following the 1976 Olympic Games, it was announced that the 1980 Olympic Games in Moscow would include Women's Hockey and Men's Hockey after an absence of many years. Thus Great Britain, for the first time, would have to select a team formally. Trials were held with players from England, Northern Ireland, Scotland and Wales and, in 1977, the first Great Britain Olympic Squad was announced. Marilyn was, of course, selected and, for the next three years, played a huge part in ensuring that Great Britain became one of only six teams to qualify for the 1980 Moscow Olympics. The political situation vis-à-vis Afghanistan resulted in the Western governments, including our own, withdrawing their teams from these Games. Thus the very real prospect of a gold medal was denied the British team, in which there were four Welsh players – Anne Ellis (Captain), Sheila Morrow, Shirley Morgan and, of course, Marilyn Pugh. It says much for her character that this huge disappointment did not affect her commitment and enthusiasm, and she continued to represent Great Britain and Wales until her retirement.

Marilyn has always been a quiet, unassuming but very committed person. Indeed, when she first came on to the Welsh scene, I thought she was extremely shy, but this was before I realised that this was due to the fact that English was her second language and that in Welsh she was far more outgoing and comfortable. She has always been very proud of her Welsh heritage, the Black Mountain and Brynaman – or 'Lower Brynaman' as she was always so quick to point out. Indeed, she was the only player to know the second verse of Calon Lân and always insisted that we sang it!

Anne Ellis

SCOTT QUINNELL

If there were any lingering doubts about whether or not Scott Quinnell could be considered one of Wales's greatest forwards, then his performance on the 2001 Lions tour to Australia will have dispelled those doubts forever

Scott was always considered to be a gifted ball carrier and his colossal frame and remarkable balance were perfectly suited to that aspect of the game. It wasn't long before these talents combined to produce one of the most memorable tries ever seen at Cardiff Arms Park. After collecting an awkward ball from his bootlaces he tore through the French defences with a mixture of speed and power a distance of 40 meters to score in the corner.

Such rare attacking ability in a man of his stature was impossible to ignore and it came as no surprise when rugby league giants Wigan approached Scott to play in their professional code.

After a relatively successful period at Wigan and several rugby league appearances for Wales, Scott was welcomed back to the newly professionalised union game and within a year he was selected to tour South Africa with the Lions. Unfortunately, injury prevented him from making a significant impact on that tour and he was forced to return home early and unfulfilled.

Four years later he was selected to tour with the Lions for a second time, and on this occasion he unequivocally carved out his position alongside Welsh rugby's most outstanding figures. His tireless contribution in the test matches will be remembered primarily for the rampaging runs through the heart of the Wallabies' defence, who soon became resigned to the fact that they simply could not stop him.

That was the defining moment in his rugby career, the moment that exorcised the doubts and ensured that once and for all, Scott Quinnell had rightfully joined that illustrious band of players that deserve the epitaph 'great'.

Gwyn Jones

PAUL RADMILOVIC

Paul Radmilovic was born on 5 March 1886 in Cardiff. The son of a Greek father and an Irish mother, he broke all records by representing Britain six times in the Olympic Games, captaining the water polo team four times. During his career he won gold medals for water polo in 1908, 1912 and 1920. In 1908 he also won the gold medal in the freestyle 4 x 200 metre relay.

His first visit to the Olympic Games was in 1906. On that occasion he reached the finals of the 100 metre and 400 metre freestyle. However, the pinnacle of his long and remarkably successful career came in the Olympic water polo final of 1920 when he scored a dramatic goal which ensured a British victory against Belgium just three minutes before the final whistle. His final appearance as a member of the water polo team was at the age of forty-two.

'Raddy' spent most of his life in Weston-Super-Mare, where he continued to swim and to compete in the local water polo team. In 1967 he was the first British swimmer to be enrolled in the Swimmers' Hall of Fame in Florida. Yet, despite winning nine ASA freestyle swimming titles, it was as a water polo player that he gained the greatest glory. Not content with his ability in the water, on dry land he was a talented golfer and footballer and also ran the Imperial Hotel at Weston. His son, who followed 'Raddy' as manager of the hotel after his death, determined that the many trophies his father had won should be put on display there for all to see how much Paul Radmilovic had achieved during his distinguished career.

Eryn White

KEVIN RATCLIFFE

During the 80s, a talented Welsh footballer distinguished himself as a defender with one of the most successful European clubs of the day. The club was Everton; the player none other than Kevin Ratcliffe.

He was born in the sleepy, little-known village of Mancott in North East Wales and unquestionably became Everton and Wales's most knowledgeable and inspirational captain. He played over three hundred games for the club as a sweeper. In 1984, at the tender age of twenty-three, Everton won the FA Cup, with Ratcliffe leading his men to a comfortable 2-0 win against Watford. He was the youngest captain to climb the thirty-nine steps at Wembley to lift the trophy since Bobby Moore, twenty-three years previously.

For a period of three seasons, Everton proved to be the most successful side in the Football League, dominating the First Division, winning the European Cup Winners' Cup and regularly appearing in the prestigious FA Cup Finals. However, there was more than a suggestion of disappointment as English sides were prevented from competing in the European Cup as a result of a firm ban which followed the Heysel disaster. If Everton had challenged the premier European sides at that time, most experts were of the same opinion; Ratcliffe's XI would have swept the others aside. They would most certainly have provided quality opposition for the Real Madrid's of the period.

As a player, Ratcliffe was unique. He possessed a brain which enabled him to be a step ahead of others; his athleticism and determination allowed him to persevere when others would have given up the ghost. He was a natural left-sided player, an immaculate passer of a football, and had that innate ability of being able to play a simple game which often out-foxed the opposition. Too often in the modern game we see individuals maintaining possession for too long a period, leading to a failure to exploit. Ratcliffe was not in this mould; he had perfected the technique of simplicity. This was the secret of his success.

He represented his country at every level and won sixty caps. He, more than any other Welshman, was desperately disappointed to miss out on qualification for European and World Cup Final stages where his talents would have been appreciated on a major stage. Since his retirement, Wales has failed to discover a player of his class and stature in defence and this has been a major weakness in the team's composition.

Whilst managing Chester FC, he showed his love and feeling for the game by paying some outstanding bills out of his own pocket. We certainly haven't heard the last of Kevin Ratcliffe.

Tomi Morgan

RAY REARDON

Happiness in 1969 Harlech consisted of two empty Corona bottles, worth 6d at Siop Gwyndy. Tough call – Elvis on Snowdon Cafe's jukebox, Batman from Maidments or the dark cool haven in the basement under the library and institute? Working men and spotty teenagers didn't mingle in coastal Meirionethshire. Only briefly at Ysgol Sul, the bandroom, whist drive or the touchline of Harlech FC home games. During daytime we were allowed into the musty slate-clad snooker room, the bastion of maleness.

Then chalking two straightish cues (with tips), unfolding the cloth, setting the table in the gloom, sliding scoreboard to zero, heads, a nod, dropping the coin into the slot, twisting the dial with a satisfying click. Twenty whole minutes of snooker, the arena lit up like White Hart Lane on cup night. 'I'll be Reardon, you be Spencer, Pullman or Davis.' Later, men arrived in overalls, cardigans and

baggy pants. Beatle-fringed teens relegated to scorers or the corner brag school. Maybe an invitation to make up a doubles team. Between shots PC 142, Twm or Dai South whispering reverentially about 'Pontins – exhibition – beat all comers – trick shots – ex-constable, ex-miner, and world champion. Ray Reardon from Tredegar down south'. Hang on, world champions came from USA, Russia or Brazil, surely?

Then BBC2 and Pot Black arrived, whispering Ted and Mr. Reardon. Always immaculately attired, waistcoat pocket for his own chalk, dramatic Dracula-like widow's peak, Brylcreem glistening under the lights and that lupine grin, the same in defeat (rarely) and victory (always). A gentleman in total command, controlling the table like a chess grand master. Relaxed, joking and avuncular until the cue slid between finger and thumb of the spread hand, staring cobra-eyed at the target ball.

A true colossus of the game – Raymond Reardon; World Champion 1970, 1973, 1974, 1975, 1976, 1978.

Philip Davies

DAI REES

Without doubt the bridesmaid of twentieth-century golf! Despite winning 28 tournaments, Dai Rees never won the one competition that was closest to his heart: the British Open Tournament. He came second three times and third once, but never came to the fore, despite leading several times at the start of the final round.

It was as if the gods were against him in that final round. For example, in 1954, needing a par to tie, his approach shot to the pin hit some grit and spun off the green; another chance lost! He is regarded as the best golfer never to have won the Open. But, above all, the name of Dai Rees is associated with the Ryder Cup.

He was the captain of the British PGA team that won the cup in 1957 after a barren period of 24 years of American dominance. For this many honours were bestowed on him, including a CBE and the BBC 'Sports Personality of the Year' award.

In total he played nine times in the Ryder Cup. This number would have been exceeded had it not been for the interruption of the war years. How many of today's players could remain at the pinnacle of their game for so long?

But golf was in Dai Rees's blood, his father also being a professional golfer. Indeed Dai was refused amateur status because of the perceived advantage given to him by his father's occupation. He learnt his trade as an assistant to his father at Aberdare Golf Club between 1929 and 1934, before becoming club professional for clubs in England.

After retirement from the tournament circuit he continued to play golf and became an avid supporter of Arsenal. It was as a result of injuries received in a car accident when returning from Highbury that ultimately led to his death aged 70 in 1983. Before Ian Woosnam, Dai Rees was the face of Welsh golf.

John Thomas

LEIGHTON REES

During my early teenage years I was a very ordinary football player and not much better when it came to rugby either. Although Phil Bennett, Gerald Davies and Mickey Thomas were heroes of mine, I couldn't relate completely to sportsmen who had been blessed with such silky skills and individual brilliance.

On the other hand there was Leighton Rees – a true Welsh great in more ways than one! Elegant – maybe not. Fit – questionable. Successful – undoubtedly! The imperfect, perfect hero to admire.

The pride an eleven-year-old boy experienced while watching The Red Dragon being held proudly aloft on television after the gentle giant had captured the first 'World Professional Darts Championship' in 1978 cannot be over-emphasised. I became even more aware of my Welshness that day. Diolch Leighton.

Fifteen years passed by before I found myself walking past the 'Leighton Rees Close' street sign and standing nervously on the doorstep of the Rees household in his beloved Ynysybwl.

Catching a glimpse of Leighton, decked out in his trademark red darts tunic in his wedding photographs wasn't the highlight of my visit, but rather the fact that an inexperienced, unknown sports reporter was given such a warm welcome in the home of a former World Champion.

Leighton Rees may not have been classed as a classic athlete, but no one can question his talent or his success in his chosen field. Although his competitive darts have gathered their fair share of dust by now, his gracious actions both on and off the 'oche' more than merit his status as a true champion.

Gwyn Derfel

DICK RICHARDSON

The title at stake – The British & Commonwealth Heavyweight Boxing Championship held at Coney Bay, Porthcawl, between our own Dick Richardson and the brute of a man from across the border, Brian London. Little did I know as a twelve-year-old on the Annual Colliers' holiday in a caravan at Trecco Bay that I would witness one of the most controversial and bizarre fights ever fought in Wales.

What I do remember was the build-up to the contest and spending a couple of afternoons in a shady gymnasium above the tombola stall at the funfair. There, Dick Richardson was going through his repertoire of sparring, punching bags and having a medicine ball thrown at his stomach.

And to the night of the fight; to see it was out of the question. For a start I couldn't afford to go; it was a sport alien to a boy brought up in the God-fearing community of Brynaman, where rugby ruled the roost. However, twiddling my thumbs in the caravan with the rain pelting down, a bored teenager got his parents' permission and a half crown to boot to spend an hour or so at the funfair.

But lo and behold! When I arrived there, to my utter disappointment, it was closed because the fun fair had been converted into an arena for the big fight. It was still raining 'cats and dogs' and I could hear a roar in the distance. I couldn't believe my luck. There were no stewards at the ticket entrance and I just managed to creep in and sit in the back row of the arena perched under the roller coaster, the figure of eight redundant for the evening.

The two boxers, London and Richardson, seemed miles away, and I could sense from the turbulent, volatile atmosphere that something untoward was going to happen. And, true to form, the two protagonists were using their tongues rather than their fists to abuse each other after the bell had rung and suddenly the ring started to fill with teenagers, trainers, bodyguards and anyone else you care to mention.

There were ten fights all at once with the fat, bald figure of Jack London, Brian's father, showing more enthusiasm for a fight than anyone else. Chaos prevailed with chairs whizzing into the ring before order was restored as both camps were escorted to the dressing rooms! The respective supporters also left in a hurry and I found myself with the pick of the ringside seats watching the supporting bouts.

And my abiding memory was the journalists around me typing a story at great speed realising that it would hit the headlines the next morning.

Who won? I think it was unfortunately Brian London!

Bleddyn Jones

SIAN ROBERTS

A recent personal interest in cycling has made me aware of the accomplishments of Sian Roberts in the developing sport of mountain biking. I recall hearing the ingratiating North Walian accent on Radio Cymru some years ago at the time that Sian was at her competitive peak but it was only in August of 1999 that I had the pleasure of meeting her at the centre that she has developed along with her husband, Dafydd, and the Forestry Commission at Coed-y-Brenin near Dolgellau.

The radio interview provided an inkling that Sian was an effusive woman, but meeting her you realise that she has boundless energy which was no doubt a driving force in her success in her field. Assessing her success in hindsight and with my own appreciation of the rigours of the sport, I have great admiration for her achievements paid for many times over in blood, sweat and laughter, since Sian is a magnetic personality bubbling with energy and smiles.

Sian switched from fell running to mountain biking in 1988 when the sport was in its infancy and quickly became British Champion both in 1991 and 1992. She achieved international status and was ranked 7th in Europe and 14th in the

World in 1994. When her sponsors pulled out the following year – a crucial pre-Olympic season – Sian was left with the unenviable dilemma of talent versus cost. Halfway through the season Sian was forced to abandon her efforts and her dream of competing in the Atlanta Olympics in 1996 – which is as much a shame to Sian as it is a shame on us as a nation that this leading sportswoman could face debt to represent her country.

No longer in competition due to injury, Sian continues to be an ambassador for the sport and has achieved as much success in the co-development of the only mountain bike 'theme park' in Britain as she did in competition itself. Along with her husband Dafydd, Sian runs a café, mountain bike hire centre and shop alongside the Forestry Commission's 'World Cup' class tracks through a beautiful area of Meirionydd. Due in part to Sian's fame in the mountain bike fraternity the centre has received greater and greater patronage over the four years of its existence, with an estimated 72,000 users in 1999 and promises of further growth in the new millennium.

Despite retirement, Sian has managed to retain her drive and enthusiasm for the sport by investing in its future at Coed-y-Brenin and therefore in the future of budding bikers at every level.

Joanna Phillips

IAN RUSH

'Milk! Yuch!'

'It's what Ian Rush drinks! And he says if you don't drink enough milk you'll end up playing for Accrington Stanley!'

Ian Rush – the man who inspired a million youngsters to drink milk. It's not the first thing that springs to mind when you think of him – but it does show his influence – if Rushy drinks it then it must be all right.

And Rushy himself was more than all right – they say that you don't realise what you've got until you've lost it and how Welsh football fans miss the sight of Rush in the Welsh shirt – the famous number nine wheeling away, arms raised to the heavens, leaving yet another keeper to pick the ball from the back of the net.

Liverpool's loss was softened by the emergence of Robbie Fowler and Michael Owen, but it's never been the same for Wales. With Rush in the team you knew that you had a chance – or more importantly if he got the chance we would score – it was as simple as that. And boy did he score, 28 international goals against some of the best teams in the world. But the statistics don't tell the whole story – no number will ever convey the emotion that swept through Cardiff Arms Park on that June night in '91, as Rush held off a challenge from Buchwald before firing the ball into the German net. 1-0 to Wales against the newly-crowned world champions – the moustachioed maestro turned away and shared the crowd's delightful disbelief.

In years to come no one will remember – or care – that he didn't score for a whole season while with Wrexham. He has nothing to prove. Wales (and Wrexham) fans will simply remember him as the greatest goal-scorer this country has ever seen – numero uno, or numero nine in his case. For that we must thank him – so I call on you all to raise a glass to Ian Rush. Mine's a pint of milk!

Dylan Ebenezer

DON SHEPHERD

Don Shepherd has always been regarded as the best county bowler never to have played for England. The Glamorgan off-spin bowler – or off-cutter as he was known because he delivered the ball quicker than a spinner – ended his career in 1972 after taking 2218 first class wickets. Unfortunately, his career coincided with some of the great England spinners such as Tony Lock, Jim Laker and Ray Illingworth, and his only recognition came with a couple of MCC tours and appearances for the Players v. Gentlemen at various festival games.

Don was first 'spotted' as a fast-medium bowler with the Fleet Air Arm at RAF Defford, a village on the outskirts of Worcester, and was immediately offered a trial by the Midlands county. But Glamorgan intervened, and, after spending a year on the MCC groundstaff in 1948, he made his county debut the following season. He took over a hundred wickets in 1952, but after experiencing a couple of lean seasons then decided to turn to off-spin, making an immediate impact. He captured 168 wickets in 1956, and went on to take over 100 wickets a season on a further eleven occasions, producing some extraordinary figures. He was virtually unplayable on rain-affected pitches recording figures of 6/5 v. Notts, 5/2 v. Leicester and 7/7 against Hampshire.

He was also an aggressive tail-ender – a typical number 10 or 11, who rarely blocked, but whose only intention was to strike the ball as hard as possible into the next parish. He entertained a capacity Bank Holiday crowd at St. Helen's in 1961, scoring a half century against Australia in only 11 scoring strokes, which included six sixes, three fours a two and a single. After retiring, Don worked at the family stores on the Gower but during the last ten years has been involved as Glamorgan's bowling coach, and he still broadcasts regularly on the county's fortunes for BBC Wales.

Edward Bevan

ALF SHERWOOD

Born in 1923, Thomas Alfred (Alf) Sherwood played for his local team Aberaman at the very young age of 14, and went on to win Welsh schoolboy honours at football and cricket playing alongside Trevor Ford and Gilbert Parkhouse. At the age of 17, he signed for Cardiff City as a wing-half and travelled twice a week after finishing his shift down the pit to train with the 'Bluebirds'. In one game Cardiff were a man short, and Sherwood was slotted into the left-back position; after a few years he made that berth his own. He had remarkable positional sense, and his pace and sureness of tackle made him one of the best defenders in the game. Stanley Matthews, the greatest of all English wingers, conceded that he always came out second-best when playing against Sherwood.

Many top clubs, including Newcastle, showed much interest in the Welsh defender, and Alf requested a transfer, but withdrew when City director Sir Herbert Merret found a good part-time job for him. He left Cardiff in 1956 after 353 appearances, and joined former City players Arthur Lever and Ken Hollyman at Newport County and made more than 200 league appearances for them also. Between 1947 and 1957 he won 41 caps for Wales, often as captain. He was known as 'the king of the sliding tackle', and in his last international he had to play in goal for his country when Welsh goalkeeper Jack Kelsey was injured and had to leave the field. In 1953 when Cardiff played Liverpool he saved a penalty from Billy Liddel.

In the 1960s he spent three seasons in New York promoting soccer, and after retiring from the game he worked for an insurance company and later for the National Coal Board. He was one of the most well liked Welsh sportsmen of his generation. He died in Cowbridge in March 1990.

Peter Hughes Griffiths

Alf Sherwood slides to perfection; Tom Finney deprived of posession.

NEVILLE SOUTHALL

'Once a bin man always a bin man!'

Not the anguished cries of Koppites frustrated by his magnificent feats on the part of their great blue rivals, but rather the playful chants of those who idolised him.

At Goodison Park they knew that Everton had never seen a goalkeeper like him and probably never would again. The same could equally be said of his country.

Neville Southall's Mersey devotees personified him in those cheeky chants. There were no frills around the best goalkeeper ever to represent Wales. Neville Southall considered himself a worker not a star. For him the job of standing between two white posts, some of the world's greatest strikes and the back of the net on the world's major stages was no different to the jobs of hod carrier and bin man as had been his lot before becoming a professional footballer. Goalkeeping was work. In his time nobody did that work before.

According to Peter Schmeichel, at his best Neville Southall was the best goalkeeper in the world. Whilst Neville himself would be the first to acknowledge the priceless contribution made at club and international level by the mesmerising speed and vision of Kevin Ratcliffe, there are few who would disagree. Folklore would have it that Neville Southall did once concede 13 goals in one game whilst representing a Llandudno Youth Team, but he went on to represent his country at the highest level 93 times, more often than anyone else in the history of Welsh football.

Neville Southall was too much of a character to be called an introvert. Yet there was a shell about him and within it he lived in his own little world. Disciplined to the point of incredulity, he was part of everything and yet quite apart. He would be the first on the bus after a game – there he would happily sit in his own company no matter how long the wait for the others to arrive from the bar. People have told the tale that immediately after an Everton victory in the Wembley FA Cup Final, his post-match celebration was to drive home immediately to his beloved North Wales rather than stay for the partying under the city lights.

His one-man protest in one of Everton's darkest periods when he opted to spend a half-time interval sitting against a post on the Goodison Park pitch rather than join his colleagues in the dressing room earned him all the wrong headlines. Yet, no one would have dared to interfere!

A compilation video of the best saves of Neville Southall would make compelling viewing. A substantial number of those saves would be saves made for Wales. No footballer wore the Welsh shirt more often or with more pride. There are precious few, if any, who were better players for their country.

One recent event served only to underline the appropriateness of those Evertonian, 'bin man' chants. Dramatically, it summed up Neville Southall. It wasn't an ordinary interview. Rather, it may have been the most important interview of his life. He stood there bathed in the sweat of anguish and disappointment following a Wales defeat at Anfield. Allowing the eye of the camera to penetrate his soul, he opened his heart and revealed that never had he held a greater ambition than to be manager of his country. A proud man, there he was, effectively on his knees in front of the viewing millions, begging for the opportunity to realise that ambition and hoping that the powers that be were listening. Neville Southall did this whilst standing in his football socks!

No one will probably ever come close to contemplating the magnitude of his disappointment when his country rejected him. One need not necessarily disagree with that ultimate decision in saying that Neville Southall of all people didn't deserve to be disappointed by Wales.

Nic Parry

MATTHEW STEVENS

Matthew Stevens is riding the crest of a wave: the quietly focused twenty-two-year-old Welsh snooker star is spearheading a renaissance in Welsh snooker. This resurgence culminated in a first all-Welsh final at the Embassy World championship in which Stevens narrowly lost a pulsating finale to his close friend Mark Williams.

This is Welsh snooker's second generation, following in the chalk marks of Ray Reardon, Doug Mountjoy and Terry Griffiths. The latter captured the World crown two decades ago, and has played a key role in nurturing Stevens's career.

Griffiths discovered Matthew as a precociously gifted nine-year-old in his matchroom snooker club in Llanelli, and retains a guiding hand and a calming influence as Stevens resolutely aims to reach the top of his profession.

He came close to conquering that summit back in April of this year, when he first appeared in his first ever World final. Stevens, the world-ranked number six, actually led 13-7 in a compelling twenty-first frame but missed the black to clear. This proved to be the defining moment of that final. Williams cleaned up and completed the next eleven of fourteen frames in imperious fashion to claim the title. It was following that defeat that Stevens received a message from World heavyweight boxing champion, Lennox Lewis. Lewis, Steven's sporting hero urged him to learn from his experience, and said that he would become World Champion soon. Rarely can there be a greater contrast between sports; Lewis's savage trade and the hypnotic hush of the green baize of the snooker table. Yet, paradoxically, they embody the same philosophies, a single-minded fear of failure, and an almost religious dedication to be the best. Their craft lies in their hands, as does their destiny.

Matthew Stevens has earned his affluence, the trappings of his success, but he remains unassuming and self-effacing. A professional since 1994, he has twice come agonisingly close to winning the United Kingdom Championship in 1998 and 1999, and it seems only a matter of time before he makes the breakthrough. He still frequents the local snooker halls and remains close to his Carmarthenshire roots. His is a prodigious talent, and yet he is a breath of fresh air in an era of sports stars whose egos outweigh burgeoning bank balances. Terry Griffiths has passed on the baton, and the cue is in safe hands.

Mark Threadgold

JIM SULLIVAN

It was 6 June, 1932. Australia and Great Britain were at it again – struggling for the Ashes, the Rugby League version, in the first test of the series at the Sydney Cricket Ground. A record crowd of 70,204 was inside the stadium. Tens of thousands were locked out in the surrounding streets. Some fans were so desperate to get a glimpse of the great match that they invaded the neighbouring Agricultural Ground and clambered on to the top of the grandstand tower.

As the match progressed, one excluded fan got some of the people inside the ground to shout down news of what was happening. Suddenly all hell was let loose as the masses inside went wild. It seemed as if the ground might erupt. Frantic with curiosity, the frustrated fan yelled up to ask if the Australians had scored. The reply that came back was, 'No, mate, Sullivan's just missed a goal!'

Jim Sullivan was so good at kicking goals it was apparently news when he missed one. In fact Sullivan was probably the goal-kicker of the millennium, in either code, in either hemisphere. Generations of rugby league followers believed Sullivan was Wales's best export and they may well have been right. He played a record 60 international matches, captaining Wales, Other Nationalities, Great Britain and even England. He captained Wigan to victory in the first Wembley Challenge Cup Final and was the first player to score in the stadium.

His middle name should have been Recordbreaker. No rugby league player has ever played as many games (928) or landed as many goals (2,867). His points tally was 6,022 (1921/46) and he kicked a century of goals in eighteen consecutive seasons. In 1925 he booted 22 goals for Wigan in a cup-tie and in 1933/34 he became the first player to score over 400 points in a season.

Oh, yes, and while I remember . . . He was also the youngest Barbarian at 17 years and 26 days of age when he played for them at Newport in 1920, and he is in the Rugby League Hall of Fame, and there is a street named after him in Wigan, and they named a bar after him at the Wigan ground, and he was featured in a postage stamp for the Rugby League Centenary in 1995, and, what's more, he only cost Wigan 750 quid. And that's only for starters!

Robert Gate

HAYDN TANNER

It is a privilege to pay tribute to one of the great sporting legends of our time – Haydn Tanner, a scrum-half who would sit comfortably with the likes of Gareth Edwards (Wales), Nick Farr-Jones (Australia), Sid Going (New Zealand) and, more recently, the current South African captain Joost Van Der Westhuizen, to name but a few outstanding players of that chosen position.

I played with Tanner for Cardiff, the Barbarians, Wales and the superb Wales Services team during World War II, when amateur and professional players shared the same rugby platform. But it was with Cardiff, during their post-war halcyon days when I was his vice-captain, that my appreciation of his immense skills as a player reached its fulfillment.

Tanner was one of the bigger scrum-halves, well capable of looking after himself in the physical content of the game. Fearless in defence, with a lightning-like service and a reverse pass that beggared belief in its speed and accuracy, Tanner was every fly-half's dream. The late and great Welsh players of the 30s; Cliff Jones, Wilfred Wooller and Arthur Rees constantly extolled his virtues as too, these days, does Billy Cleaver, Tanner's Wales and Cardiff partner for three seasons during the late 40s.

Tanner had an uncanny eye for an opening which he exploited to deadly effect but in the opinion of some critics he was not selfish enough in this aspect of his play, and I put this down to his belief that rugby football is a fifteen-a-side game, with the movement of the ball amongst forwards and backs paramount for spectator and player enjoyment.

Let me describe Tanner at his best: the occasion was the Barbarians v. Australia match at Cardiff in 1948, the game that set a precedent for the future. Tanner broke from a scrum just inside the Australian half of the field. He passes to Tommy Kemp; Kemp hands on to me, and I feed Billy Cleaver who makes ground and returns to me. I, in turn, pass to Martin Turner and, just as it appears that the attack is bound to die out, Tanner (who started it all from the left) appears outside Turner on the right wing to cross for a gem of a try; quite brilliant, and it brought the house down!

Haydn Tanner was just seventeen when he helped Swansea defeat Jack

Manchester's 1935 All Blacks and was also at the base of the scrum when Wales claimed their scalp in an Arms Park thriller later on. But for the war, he would have won infinitely more than his 25 caps and toured more than the once to South Africa in 1938 with the British Lions.

Bleddyn Williams

CLEM THOMAS

It seems that the Gilbert Match ball left the ground in R. C. C. Thomas's car! – Barbarians v. All Blacks, 1954.

Halfway up the hill from St Helen's is not a place you choose to stop. The Mumbles is obscured by houses thrown up and together. Not even Swansea's infamous city planners could have come up with this layered drabness. Far below the floodlights, I listen to Clem's latest thoughts on the state of world rugby. He is recently back from the Southern Hemisphere and is in a reflective mood.

The invective and the stories are as sharp as ever but the delivery is laboured. Illness has long taken its toll. The words flow but he leans against the railings trying to hide his long intakes of breath. After a while the words stop. He smiles on seeing my concern. Clem's house in De La Beche Street seems far away.

As the minutes pass, our talk is of Brynaman in the 50s, my childhood and Clem's glory days. We remember friends and family. We laugh about a day at his father's slaughterhouse where a father and son too alike not to argue end up fighting like brothers. The international rugby player drops like a shot bullock from a punch to the midriff. He talks about what rugby gave him, the friends, the travel, the fun. I am again with the aggressive and mobile forward who terrorised, deliberately, opposing outside-halves. I see the world-class number seven that the grainy film archives hide. I see the thinking rugby player who led Swansea and Wales and should have led the Lions. I am again with the fast-driving fast-living man about town, anyone's town. In life, as in rugby, Clem was throughout a man ahead of his time.

Eventually we part. Clem restarts his slow journey home. I watch for a while, reminded that we should not let our heroes and our great men grow old. Their skills and their achievements stay with us. It is our loss that we forget.

Ron Jones

DAVID THOMAS

Ask any golfer of whatever standard what he or she would like to do more than anything else and I bet most would answer, 'Hit it a damn sight further than I do now.' It was that ability to drive the ball vast distances by virtue of timing, technique and applied strength that made Dave Thomas stand out amongst his golfing peers.

Born in Newcastle, his father had played rugby for Wales and his mother was Britain's foremost woman snooker player, so it was little wonder that the young Thomas would excel at sport. He left school early to join the professional ranks, and soon made his mark as an assistant and then on the ever developing European Golf Tour circuit.

'If only he could chip he would be a world beater,' – how many times did I as a young golf fanatic read that about Dave Thomas as I pored avidly over every golf magazine and book I could find. Plagued by the equivalent of the dreaded 'yips' with his short game and hampered by a troublesome back injury, he never really reached the dizzy heights that his undoubted talent deserved, but he still managed to be runner up in the British Open twice, win three different Opens in Europe, represent Great Britain in the Ryder Cup on four occasions, Wales in the Canada (World) Cup ten times and just for good measure to be British Match Play Champion. If only he could chip!!

As a youngster I was taken by Meirion Kyffin, a kindly senior member of my home golf club at Aberystwyth, to see the British Open at Royal Birkdale in the 60s, and it was there that I saw the tall, bespectacled figure of Dave Thomas for the first time. His driving was awesome; he was undoubtedly the John Daly or Tiger Woods of his day. I was totally mesmerised, and when I got home I begged my parents to get me a set of Goudie 'Dave Thomas' clubs believing, mistakenly as it turned out, that some of Thomas's magical power would be transferred to me if only I had a set of his autographed clubs.

Years went by before I saw the big man again, so you can imagine my delight when, while I was a member of BBC Wales Sports Department, its then Head, Onllwyn Brace, asked me to go and film an interview with him at the Belfry – home of many dramatic Ryder Cup encounters. By now he was a respected golf course designer and he spoke eloquently to Peter Walker about his hopes for the Belfry and about his future course design projects.

As I watched and listened, I marvelled. Here at last I had been given the opportunity to meet one of my all-time golfing heroes, Dave Thomas, the gentle Welsh giant. Big of stature, big with talent. In every sense, I have always looked up to him.

Geraint Evans

IWAN THOMAS

European and Commonwealth Champion; World Cup and European Cup medallist; Olympic silver medallist; World Championship silver medallist . . . not a bad record for a Social Secretary of a University athletics team. And that's how I first met Iwan Thomas. Brunel University, then known as West London Institute, and previously Borough Road College, is one of the foremost athletics institutions in Britain. Its alumni include Alan Pascoe, Kathy Cook née Smallwood, Mark Taylor and Nigel Bevan, along with two other notable sporting stars: Steve Fenwick and Elgan Rees.

Even as a student, Iwan was a reasonably well-known and recognisable athlete. I had been introduced to him by the university's infamous figure, Mr. Charles Lipton. He was most approachable and likeable and soon became a bosom pal. The friendship allowed me to join in some regular hill sessions in Richmond Park. Anyone reading this and who has used 'hill sessions' as part of a training routine, will know that they can be quite demanding and occasionally quite stomach churning and gut wrenching. Horrendous is the word. This was true of most weeks spent during the winter in the vicinity of Richmond.

Iwan, as with all other international athletes, trains at a very high intensity. Spending time with such people helps to develop a tough and seasoned mental approach, and if there had been an international event based in and around Richmond Hill, I would have been there or thereabouts contesting for a medal. I felt that confident. I was being inspired by a superstar; my level of fitness had improved substantially.

One training programme does stick in the memory. A Tuesday afternoon in February, damp, dismal and depressing. The session was pretty demanding. I think it was a combination of something like ten or twelve runs of various lengths. We commented at the time that it was quite unusual that no one was sick after completing the schedule. After warming down, we made our way back to the car contemplating a mug of hot chocolate and a soak in the bath. Five minutes into the journey, I had to ask Iwan to pull over, got out of the car in record time and proceeded to regurgitate the contents of my lunch down a drain at the side of the road. The side of his car was also damaged (I still haven't told him!). On getting back into the vehicle I was congratulated on a 'good session'! I don't think he would have been so complimentary had he known I'd thrown up down the side of his sponsored car. It's not the most pleasant of claims to fame, but how many of you can truly claim that you've been congratulated on being sick over an Olympic medallist's car . . . by the Olympian himself! Iwan Thomas; outstanding athlete, outstanding person.

Rowan Griffiths

JOHN GREGORY THOMAS

Much like the seemingly intractable wartime code that was 'enigma', so too our very own Greg Thomas – enigmatic. Brilliant, precocious with raw talent in abundance, and yet possessing that fatal flaw that straddles greatness and frustrating unfulfilled ambition – thus was Glamorgan's exocet of the 80s.

In actual terms, the first-class analysis is not particularly impressive. His career spanned 1979-1991, during which time he played 106 matches, scored 8419 runs, including two centuries, claimed 525 wickets at a strike rate of 31.05, and took 74 catches. He did not become a regular until 1984, was dogged by injury and was not capped until 1986, and he actually failed to take 50 championship wickets in any of his playing seasons. Why then does the memory of Gregory Thomas's Glamorgan playing days, some 20 years on, still trigger debate, but also a universal recognition of short-lived greatness?

Greg represented a pre-automaton sporting era. He was pacey, erratic and loose. He was the George Best and Stan Collymore of cricket. After having come through the Glamorgan Second XI championship academy that included the likes of Hugh Morris, he earned rave reviews for his speed and aggression in South Africa. After years of tacit acceptance that all quickies hail from the Caribbean, to discover that the 'fastest white bowler on earth' came from Trebannws, spoke Welsh and played for Glamorgan, was quite inspirational for all Welsh cricket followers at that time. Of course, in keeping with the age, he was controversial before Boycott and Botham made controversy their own goal standard. One recalls in 1985 at Southampton when Glamorgan were playing Hampshire on an easy paced wicket and where Greg achieved uncanny pace and lift, giving Gordon Greenidge a great deal of discomfort and a normally calm Mark Nicholas heart palpitations. In came the late and great Malcolm Marshall to a reception party of 90 miles per hour projectiles whistling past his face. Greg was clearly fired up and after serving up yet another snorter, he glared down the wicket and taunted the great Marshall – 'Come on Marshy; you don't like it when it's up your nose, do you?'

His talent could not even escape the England selectors, usually so focused on the Home Counties, who installed him as strike bowler for the 1985 winter tour of the West Indies. His first ball in test cricket almost produced the scalp of the majestic Desmond Haynes and but for a dropped gulley catch by Willey from his second delivery, Greg could have had the most dramatic of introductions to test cricket. Wickets did come his way, however, and he took 8 wickets in the first three tests. A below par Thomas performance in the fourth test cost him his place in the last test, which England duly lost, thereby initiating the unwelcome 5-nil blacklash tag.

Greg's scrapes with West Indies cricketers continued, however. In 1987, with Glamorgan bottom of the championship table, and taking on Viv Richards's sunset at Taunton, Greg got the responsive wicket that he so coveted. The Trebannws wizard sent the leather whizzing and pinging about King Viv's swaying body, which ultimately prompted Greg to follow through down the wicket, glare at the great man and declare, 'It's red, it's round and it's fast – try hitting it.'

Nonchalant, powder keg Viv calmed himself, steadied the ship, and two overs later stepped to leg and crashed Greg into the River Tome. The Wrigley induced jaw movement and careful prodding of the crease prefaced the riposte, 'Well, man. You know what it looks like; now go get it.'

Sadly, the recurrence of a longstanding pelvic injury forced Greg into permanent retirement in 1991. By then, of course, he had left Glamorgan some three years earlier, seeking more responsive wickets to bolster his England claims, but not before creating an indelible impression as a great Welsh fast bowler whose cameos will remain forever.

Owain Llywelyn

PARRY THOMAS

We were heading for Cardiff, Siân and I, with our ever-inquisitive youngest son in the back. We had just climbed the Nant-y-Caws Hill when a shout came from the rear, 'What's that there?' And on a garage forecourt on our left stood a trailer carrying a blue and white racing car, its long pointed tail aiming straight at us.

'Babs!' I shouted, just as excited as the child. 'That's Babs!' And I knew that there would be peace and quiet no longer. I would have to spill the beans. And at once I was back in Cardigan School, hearing my friend Denzil Thomas's stories of the Pendine Races. They were second or third hand, admittedly, but, for that very reason, all the more intriguing.

Rhys, Denzil's father, worked as a mechanic for Arthur Brough, owner and designer of the Brough Superior – a 1000cc motorbike, and one of the fastest in the country at that time. Indeed, Rhys had driven the bike himself, at speeds of over 120 mph, over the Flying Mile – which was very close to the record of the time. Sometime later, I saw that bike in pieces in the Dyffryn Barn.

Be that as it may, Rhys knew his stuff. He was on Pendine Beach that fateful day; March the 4th, 1927. There had been rumours for weeks that Parry Thomas intended to make an attempt at the world record any day, before Seagrave could bid for glory over in Daytona, America. The weather had been against him, however, and he himself was suffering with 'flu.

After having postponed more than once, Babs had already been close to the record that morning, and the mechanics had been tinkering with the car's set-up before another attempt could be made. But something broke on the car's driving chain, and apparently, Parry Thomas put his head out through the door in order to see what was wrong. It was at that exact moment that the chain snapped, hitting him and killing him instantly.

Babs was buried at the beach and forty years passed before I set eyes again on the object of that great tragedy.

Dic Jones

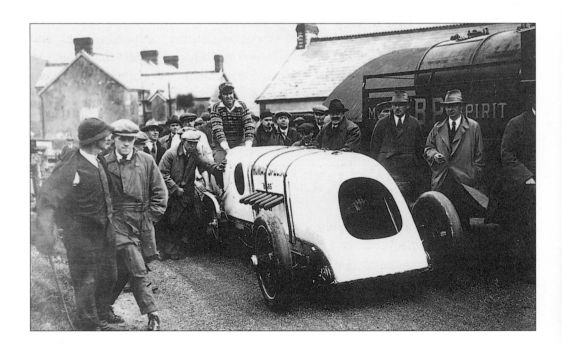

TANNI GREY THOMPSON

'Hello! How are you? You're my heroine you know.' I cringe with embarassment every time I see a picture of or hear Tanni Grey's name mentioned. These were the words that spilt forth when I first met the lady. Well, what else would you say to someone who has won nine Olympic gold medals and five World Championship gold medals in the 100, 200, 400 and 800 metre track events? The only thing I can say in my defence is that my remarks broke the ice, as it were, and our relationship started on the right note.

Tanni is, it seems, always in the public eye. She attracts media attention wherever she goes and her wedding was even featured in *Hello* magazine! This fame has not, however, altered her personality in any way. She is always open, cheery and has a very positive outlook on life.

Does all the fame and glory come at a price, I asked. 'Not really,' she answered. 'It's easy for me because I love what I do. I've never had to sacrifice anything, although my family have'. I asked whether she wished things were different. She answered firmly, 'No'. She would be the same person even if she wasn't in a wheelchair. Her motivation lies in winning. Winning a gold medal still gives her a buzz, which is why she keeps going.

Her career started when she came under the influence of an inspirational and understanding Physical Education teacher. Having been in a wheelchair since she was seven, she attended a mainstream comprehensive school but was unaware that she could attend normal PE classes. After watching her friends one week she was told to bring her swimming costume in future as there was no reason why she couldn't join in. After that she never looked back.

Leisa Davies

MAURICE TURNBULL

Maurice Turnbull was one of the greatest names in Welsh sport during the 1930s. A superb all-round sportsman, he played county cricket for Glamorgan, Test cricket for England, and both international rugby and hockey for Wales. He also played club rugby and hockey for Cardiff, won cricket and hockey Blues whilst up at Cambridge University, won the South Wales Squash Championships, had an interest in horse racing, was a fine Bridge player and was a lover of good wines, poetry and music.

It was whilst leading Glamorgan during the 1930s that Turnbull really made a name for himself. He thrilled the crowds with his dashing strokeplay and was a fine enough leader to be regarded as the best captain in county cricket who never led England in Tests. Behind this glittering sporting career lay a true gentleman, and one with a strong character, clarity of thought, powers of organisation and shrewd decision-making. All of this was clearly evident in the way he successfully carried out his duties as Secretary of Glamorgan, as a Test Selector for England, and in the business world of South Wales.

He also had a devout Catholic faith, and, after being educated at Downside School, it was this deep faith which helped him as he fought many battles on and off the field. Together with his good friend, Johnnie Clay, Turnbull strove to gain higher recognition for Glamorgan, and to dispel their image as a ragbag eleven and an easy pushover in Championship cricket. He generously gave his time and money to the organisation of fund-raising activities for the county, and his efforts guaranteed the survival of the club, and paved the way for their eventual rise to the Championship title in 1948.

Turnbull also fought to retain the services of several cricketers, who in the fullness of time blossomed into talented players, whilst on the sports field, both at home and abroad, he represented Wales and England, and typically led from the front. Yet in a more bloody battle in Normandy during the Second World War, Maurice Turnbull was to pay the highest price, giving his life for King and Country, whilst serving as a Major in the Welsh Guards. Even in these final grim moments, Turnbull was as always leading by example, and bravely leading a counter-attack on German troops when he was tragically killed.

Andrew Hignell

KIRSTY WADE

Kirsty's parents, Chris and Frank McDermott, relate a tale about the occasion Kirsty ran her first race in the infants' school sports. Having run three quarters of the course, she stopped, looked back at her fellow competitors, beckoned them on, and then joined them in crossing the finishing line. Although her natural running talent was apparent in those early days, little did her parents think on that occasion that their young daughter was destined to win gold medals and international honours for her country.

Her talent was put to the test for the first time in 1975 when, as a junior pupil at Llandrindod High School, she was selected to represent Powys in the Welsh Schools' Track and Field Championships in the 800m event. She won the race in a faster time than that recorded by the winner of the Middle Girls' race, resulting in her being selected to run for the Welsh Schools' team in the British Schools' International Championships. That was her first taste of success on the athletics field and the career of Kirsty McDermott (as she was then known) as a middle distance runner had been firmly launched.

Her progress was rapid. In 1976 she became the Welsh Schools' Cross Country champion, and won both the 800m and Long Jump in the Schools Championships. Later in the year she became the British Junior 800m Champion, winning in a new record time. In recognition of her successes she was awarded the BBC/*Western Mail* Junior Sports Personality of the year.

At the age of 14 she was ranked No 1 in the UK junior rankings and No 1 in the Senior Welsh Women's rankings! The Welsh Schools' Middle Girls' 800m record she set in 1977 still stands to this day!

In 1978 she captained the Schools' team and added the 800m title to her list of achievements. In the same year she won an Athletics Scholarship to Millfield School.

Kirsty had now established herself as the greatest prospect at 800m that Wales had ever seen. This was soon to be proved correct. In 1982 she became the first Welsh woman to win a gold medal at the Commonwealth Games. Four years later, at Edinburgh, she became the first person to win the 800m crown twice and also the first woman to win a double Gold – at 800m and 1500m. In the same year she wrote herself into the record book yet again by becoming the first woman to win the BBC/*Western Mail* Sports Personality of the Year.

Tesni Davies

NIGEL WALKER

Vibrant and exciting – two adjectives one can use to describe Wales as it enters the twenty-first century. Currently, the country seems to be thriving; Wales is fashionable and in the public eye. The land of song is now characterised, not by the booming chapel tones of Cwm Rhondda, but by 'preachers' from Blackwood and 'furry animals' from Bethesda.

Wales's most famous sons, when it comes to individual heroism in song and sport, are Tom Jones and Lynn Davies. The roots of the current boom in 'Cool Cymru' is hard to define. In the same way as the new wave of rock artists benefited from the inroads made by an underrated crew of West Walians called 'Gorky's Zygotic Mynci', the crop of extremely talented Welsh athletes such as Colin Jackson and Jamie Baulch could probably trace their inspiration back to the time when Nigel Walker broke through as a serious contender.

It is inevitable that comparisons will be made between Walker and Jackson. They are both close friends and were training partners. Jackson will always gain the upper hand if comparisons are to be made; he was Commonwealth Champion, World Champion and at one time had run the 110 metre hurdles faster than anyone else. Walker, however, competed at the 1984 Los Angeles Olympics getting to the semi-finals and won medals galore up to and including European Championship standard.

Being an athlete was probably the worst crime Nigel Walker could have committed as he decided to embark on a new career and wear the blue and black shirt of Cardiff RFC. 'He can't possibly read the game, his defence will be tested,' were the words uttered and printed by a blinkered majority. No one referred to the possibility of a Michael Jordan-esque ability of receiving the ball and creating mayhem in an organised defence. No, that wasn't a consideration because his rugby brain hadn't been developed. Incredibly, all this took place when rugby players in Wales showed almost 'nil' excitement on the rugby pitch. We needed a lift, we needed to escape from the desolate Sarahan 80s. In fact, when Nigel Walker scored a 90yard screamer against Newport at Rodney Parade, it was the first time I swore in front of my father and got away with it!

Trystan Bevan

PETER WALKER

I believe the seed was sown when I was around seven years of age. In those days we did not own a car, and so it was only the most committed follower who would make the one and a half hour bus journey from Garnant to St Helen's to watch Glamorgan play cricket. I still cannot decide if my father was enlightened and believed in sexual equality or deep down thought that his only child was indeed a boy who would grow to love the game as much as he did.

Whatever his reasons, the treks to Swansea were made with alarming regularity. Once the initial boredom had worn off and I was now a pimply teenager, I gradually realised that those men in white were in fact MEN and some of them were indeed good-looking men. These were the days of Pressdee, Parkhouse, the Jones brothers and, my favourite, Peter Walker.

He was tall, he was slim, he possessed awesomely fast reflexes and was an athletic bowler – what else could a girl want!! These were the days when St Helen's would be packed on an August Bank Holiday for the visiting Australians, West Indians or whoever happened to be the visitors that year. Simpson, Redpath, O'Neill, Sobers; they were all there in turn, but none possessed the qualities of Walker!

Time has now moved on. I have graduated from being a Junior to a Premier Club Member and go to the matches voluntarily. What wouldn't I give to see that tall, gangly figure throwing himself around in the leg trap, bounding in to bowl or striding out to bat. Yes, we could do with some of his class in the team of 2002.

Jill Bevan

CYRIL WALTERS

Cyril Walters, the former Glamorgan, Worcestershire and England batsman, died in hospital in Neath on December 23rd 1992. Walters had been one of the most elegant and consistent opening batsmen in county cricket in the early 1930s and held the distinction of being the first Welshman to captain England, having led the side against Australia at Trent Bridge in the first Test of the summer of 1934, Bob Wyatt having broken his thumb.

Born in Bedlinog on August 28th, 1905, Cyril Walters first came to prominence as a stylish batsman and nimble rugby player at Neath Grammar School. His prowess at schoolboy level drew the attention of the Glamorgan selectors, who were keen to introduce young home-grown talent into their fledgling county side. After impressing the Captain, 'Tal' Whittington, Walters was drafted into their side for the match against Lancashire at Cardiff Arms Park in June 1923. It was an inauspicious debut, however, as Walters managed just 1 and 12, but he continued to be a heavy scorer at school and club levels, and made six further appearances for Glamorgan later in the season.

Walters's athletic prowess in the field also attracted the eye of the county selectors, who were aware of the presence of many ageing amateurs in the Welsh side, and consequently young Cyril played in all of Glamorgan's Championship matches in 1924. He scored his maiden century against Warwickshire at Swansea and, a fortnight later, hit an unbeaten 114 against Leicestershire on the same ground.

Like Maurice Turnbull, his partner in the Glamorgan middle order, Walters was seen as having a big future with the Welsh club, but the young architect and surveyor was keen to develop his business career and seek some security, and after just six matches in 1927, he accepted a business offer and 'retired' from the county game. However, at the end of that summer he accepted the post of Secretary at Worcestershire and joined the Midlands county, for whom he made 137 appearances up until 1935.

Walters's switch to New Road was a turning point in his career as he moved up to open the innings, improving his technique after coaching from 'Tiger' Smith. Despite his slight physique, Walters proved himself a reliable performer and displayed an elegant, wristy style against the new ball. His move to the Midlands also opened other new doors for him and he took over the Worcestershire captaincy in 1931, impressing with his cool leadership.

1933 was his best season, when he hit a career-best 226 against Kent at Gravesend, created a Worcestershire record of nine centuries and 2292 runs, and was one of Wisden's Five Cricketers of the Year. In the same year he was also promoted to the England test side for the first match against the West Indies. He marked his debut with a typically composed 51, and kept his place for the rest of the series, as well as for the winter tour of India under the captaincy of Douglas Jardine. Walters adapted well to the slower pitches and developed his footwork against spin bowling, scoring 102 (his only Test century) in the third Test at Madras.

During the Ashes series of 1934, Walters also developed a solid opening partnership with Herbert Sutcliffe, and scored 82, 52, 50 and 64 in four of his eight innings for England that summer. His average of 52.26 showed that he had comfortably bridged the gap between county and Test cricket. He announced his retirement in 1935 after a series of small injuries and a certain amount of domestic pressure. As he modestly admitted in an interview in December 1986, 'I couldn't go on playing for ever. I really had to do something else.'

Andrew Hignell

STEVE WATKIN

Picture a school built high on the mountainside of a densely-forested, steep-sided valley. Part of the school is typical of many in Wales. The classrooms built in a long, continuous line, using sandstone which had been cut into shape. Larger white/grey masonry formed great archways above every entrance into the institution. The rest of the school is characteristic of 60s and 70s architecture; reinforced concrete, flat roofs and building bricks. The modern buildings towered over the individual, and this, coupled with the aggressive countenance of the squat, old section and the forest setting, formed an imposing sight for any new pupil. It looked more like Dracula's castle than a place of learning.

Of all the developments at the school, the most useful was the large Dutch barn. Fifty metres long by twenty-five in width, its uneven tarmac playing-surface is sunk deep between two long concrete terraces. In winter it's Cardiff Arms Park, Llynfi Road or the Vetch, while in summer it would be converted into St Helen's or Lords. On this particular day however, it was definitely a hostile Sabina Park, as the schoolboys of Croeserw Primary School were taking on a second year side from Cymer Afan while on a day visit to the comprehensive.

It's June 1978, and the rain, as usual, is torrential. Water cascades down the terracing as it gushes down from the adjacent mountainside, forming pools in the patches where the tarmac is missing. Due to the lack of fluorescent bulbs the light is appalling, but despite the difficulties, the boys are playing cricket. The youngsters from Croeserw had the audacity to dismiss the older lads quite cheaply, and were well on the way to surpassing their target, until a tall, lanky lad called 'Banger' began to bowl. One by one, even two by two, the wickets fell as this 'white West Indian' put the fear of God into them.

Sitting on one of the few dry patches on the terracing, nervously awaiting his turn to bat, was a short rotund figure. He didn't particularly want to wield his willow wand in anger and hoped, nay prayed, for his team mates to exceed the total and save him from what would surely be the agony of batting. Suddenly, the sound of a ball crashing against aluminium wickets echoed around the barn. With all the enthusiasm of a French aristocrat going to have his hair cut by Monsieur Guillotine, the little batsman trudges the fifteen yards out to the middle.

With the bat firmly gripped in his sweaty palms, he trembles uncontrollably as this paler version of Joel Garner begins his run up. His run up is all of 10 yards, and he releases the white rubber missile at an immense speed. The young batsman bravely plays a forward defensive about ten seconds after the ball passes him. Forgetting that the ball is made of rubber, he is unaware of the fact it has rebounded off the wall behind him, and the ball returns, hitting him on the back of the head. Shaken and somewhat dazed, the batsman is lifted to his feet by 'Banger', who, when assured that the kid was OK, resumed his bowling stint.

'He seems a nice bloke,' the little boy thought, but that impression was quickly

157

dispelled, as the next delivery came even more quickly and seemingly at chest height. Our wood-wielding Zorro backs away from his wicket in a desperate attempt to make room for himself so he can masterfully cut the ball into a pool of water just behind point (that's my version and I'm sticking to it). The ball smashes against the undefended wickets and the disappointed (but relieved) youngster returns to his spot on the terracing.

This story is in no way fabricated. The 'white West Indian' is, of course, Steve Watkin, while the short, rotund kid was yours truly. I can't decide what had the biggest impact on me. Was it the five years in the renowned Cricket Academy of Cymer Afan Comprehensive or the two balls, the only two balls, that I've ever faced off Steve Watkin? Since that day, my opinion of Steve has remained the same; a great bloke to speak to at close quarters when he's picking you up after hitting you, at a dinner table or over a pint in the bar, but definitely one to be avoided at the longer range of around twenty-two yards. It was those two deliveries that encouraged me to abandon the idea of playing cricket and to concentrate on rugby instead (my success with the oval ball being equally disastrous).

However, when involved in cricket, I made sure that I was always on his side, and to be absolutely certain, I followed Steve to Maesteg CC. It was here that Steve broke into the league scene and flourished, while I excelled in the relative safety of the score box or bar. At the 'Old Parish' he took 263 league wickets in just six seasons, including a club record 68 in the 1985 season, breaking the 30 year old previous best set by Maesteg legend Moss Walters and former Glamorgan and Middlesex bowler Norman Hever. During this period, Steve was recognised by Glamorgan, and the rest, as they say, is history, as he travelled along the hard road towards becoming a professional, international sportsman in perhaps the hardest of games. A case of triumph over adversity if ever there was one.

The Afan Valley is hardly the place that springs to mind when thinking of areas that produce Test Cricketers. The geography of the area prevents cricket from progressing, so football, rugby and cross country running are the main sports in this wonderful part of the world. Steve didn't have well-prepared practice wickets or state of the art facilities in his early years. No. Steve's cricket environment was a Dutch barn, rugby pitch, a field in a Duffryn affectionately known as the "Cabbage Patch" or a gravel tennis court. That perhaps has been the making of him.

Steve has risen to the top despite these factors, making his achievement all the more remarkable. He has succeeded because of his immense courage, determination and willingness to learn. He is a model to all aspiring young sportsmen. He had to be a bowler though. Well, would you fancy batting on any of the aforementioned surfaces? A delivery which lifts viciously after pitching on the edge of a piece of worn tarmac, place-kickers' mount or on a conveniently placed cowpat would be enough to unnerve any batsman!

The great thing about Steve is that he hasn't changed a bit. He always has time for people whether they are from his past or if he is meeting them for the first time. Because of this he had endeared himself to everyone who has come into contact with him. Everybody speaks highly of this great man.

Dave Berry

ALLAN WATKINS

Allan Watkins was the glory of Glamorgan's leg trap and the despair of physicists. They say that many chaps festooned with MSc, PhD and the like retired to monasteries after witnessing catches the finest scientific opinion declared impossible.

Dennis Compton defied logic; Gary Sobers slaughtered probability; Watkins wrecked every law of aerodynamics. A body moving through air, this branch of science insists, is subject to drag. That's why they make fast things pointy.

Watkins was never pointy. He was, to be blunt, blunt. Just as well: any quicker and he'd have been catching blokes before they got to the wicket.

He made his maiden hundred against Surrey in 1946, at the first game of cricket I ever saw. It was years before anyone could convince me that he wasn't better than Don Bradman. They still have their work cut out when I remember pull-drives like Thor's hammer.

But even if I now concede that he was not the all-time No 1 batsman (though his Test average of 40.50 beats W. G. Grace and Frank Woolley) or bowler (wicked in the right conditions, mind), this is beyond dispute: at short fine leg he was unsurpassable.

If you think you know of a better one, order DNA tests to discover his planet of origin. Watkins took catches you had to see to believe; even then you wondered. And maybe his finest was the catch that never was.

The scene: Merthyr. *The occasion*: charity game. *State of play*: local side being dismantled. Inside edge off swiftish one. Ball flies ant's kneecap-high. Watkins, even less pointy by now, makes light look a slowcoach as he dives to hold it at full stretch.

Turns left hand, flicks ball to boundary. Rises. 'Would have been a great catch if I'd held on,' he grins. Watching physicists weep softly, and beg for the addresses of monasteries.

Alun Rees

DAVID WATKINS

David Watkins has to rank as one of the most exhilarating outside halves ever produced in Wales. At a time when the outside-half factory was flourishing, succeeding Cliff Morgan and preceding Barry John (just) and Phil Bennett, Watkins will be remembered as one of the best.

Jet propelled he certainly was as he skimmed over even the muddiest of surfaces without a hand being laid on him. He enjoyed a distinguished career, his crowning moment with Newport coming in that memorable victory over the All Blacks in 1963. He became a Wales regular as well, terrorising defences at international level in his 21 appearances for his country. But what distinguished Watkins from so many of Wales's outside-halves was that, having achieved everything the game could offer at union, including captaining the British Lions, he proceded to do the same in rugby league.

He made the plunge and changed codes, deciding to join Salford. Far from being overwhelmed, he went on to crack records in the league game as well. For a slight outside half, his ability to take a knock was remarkable and his defensive prowess set him apart.

He broke the league goal-kicking record with Salford, for whom he also broke the record for consecutive appearances. And he went on to captain both Wales and the British rugby league teams, becoming the first player to lead Britain in both codes.

Going back to union, he achieved so much in the game, troubling so many defences with his blinding pace and elusiveness, despite the fact that, in those days, the outside-half usually received the ball and the opposing wing-forward at roughly the same time. He enjoyed many tussles with the tearaway wing-forwards of his time notably Haydn Morgan, Dai Hayward, Omri Jones and Alan Dix.

Hand on heart, David would admit that they all troubled him, but tie him down? No one ever did that. He has been Newport rugby club chairman for the past seven years, serving initially through troubled times as the team slid from the glory days he so enriched.

But today the club is reviving, with some big names on board, and hopes are high that some great times are just around the corner, with one of Newport's most famous sons at the helm.

Robin Davey

FREDDIE WELSH

On 29 July 1927, the body of one of the world's greatest ever boxers was found in a low-rent New York apartment. The NYPD officers trawled through the scant possessions of Freddie Welsh, expecting to piece together yet another rags-to-riches-to-rags-again tale. But it quickly became apparent that this was no Greek tragedy with gloves.

Frederick Hall Thomas was born the son of a well-to-do auctioneer in Pontypridd. A sickly child, Freddie developed signs of consumption, and as a young boy was sent to the sunshine of California. His physician prescribed pugilism as the ideal exercise to strengthen the frail young Welshman. To the doctor's astonishment, the rich kid was a natural. Frederick had found his true calling. He knew that this was a game that would not only improve his health but also his bank balance.

Boxing was big business in America at the turn of the twentieth century and the only person standing between the young Welshman and a prize-fighting fortune was his mother. Nice middle-class boys didn't punch for a living, so Frederick Hall Thomas became Freddie Welsh.

The family in Pontypridd was oblivious to the fact that Freddie Welsh was quickly becoming one of the leading lightweights in America. All was progressing smoothly for Welsh until news came from Pontypridd that his mother was dying. He sailed for home but news of his boxing exploits arrived in Britain before him and the National Sporting Club in London soon ensured that Freddie Welsh was fighting and beating the best lightweights in Britain.

Welsh had not only learned how to box in America but also the art of maximising his purse. He would take on two fighters a night and only take the prize money if he knocked out both men – which he did every time. Welsh continued winning until eventually he relieved world champion Willie Richie of his lightweight title. He returned to America but the Great War denied him the opportunity of cashing in as champion of the world.

Welsh did make enough money to buy a health farm but then the Depression intervened and his business and money were gone. Amid rumours of suicide, Freddie Welsh, one of the greatest lightweights to step into a ring, died alone, a broken man.

Andrew Gallimore

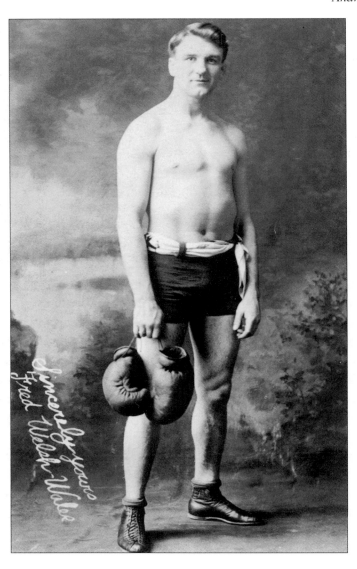

HELEN WESTON

I have known Helen all her life, as our families lived near each other and I was in the same class at school as her brother Paul. Little did I think then how our lives would become intertwined so many years later!

Helen first played netball for Wales on 22nd November 1982 against New Zealand, in Cardiff. A fresh seventeen year old, admired by many for her skills and ability to read the game, not least by her father, himself an International basketball player and referee; he has followed her career ever since. It has spanned four World Championships, a World Games, a Commonwealth Games and a year of International matches, so far, Helen has 107 International caps.

One match sticks in my mind – played in February 1997 in Northern Ireland. We needed to win, our record against NI over recent years was mixed and the pressure was on Wales. The match started fast and furious, NI had the lead at quarter time 6-15. By half time, the lead had changed hands several times, but still NI were up 27-25. Third quarter early on Wales pulled ahead by two but the determined Irish fought back, levelled and snatched two goals to end the third quarter 40-38. Final score: NI 49; Wales 54, a turnaround that can only be put down to the Welsh defence, who drove forward, picking off interception after interception, allowing the ball to move into attack for a goal. It was the best nailbiting netball quarter I have ever watched. Helen was outstanding; her determination to succeed, her longstanding ability to read the game, and her level-headed approach came to the fore. Winning that game, in the final quarter, was the first step to Wales's participation in the 1998 Commonwealth Games.

Sue Holvey

JIMMY WILDE

It is the week before Christmas. Thick fog surrounds Holborn Stadium in London. Lamps had been lit since the early afternoon. The metallic sound of trams on their tracks, the sound of horses' hooves, the sound of thousands of feet on the street. Men with cloth caps and mufflers. The smell of beer and cigarettes. Busy bookies from Bermondsey and Bow. The rich Jews of Golders Green, coats with astrakhan collars. The smell of cigars. Soldiers from the trenches of Flanders in khaki.

In the bowels of the stadium, the Welshman is the irritable Jimmy Wilde; a thin, pale boxer, five feet and three inches tall. He was to have fought at two o'clock in the afternoon. It's now a quarter to four. White tiles, buckets, the smell of sweat, blood and ointment. The previous bout has just finished. He's climbing the stairs lightfootedly with Teddy Lewis, his manager, carrying his small bag.

The thousands in Holborn are screaming. Jimmy Wilde is the hero. Everyone wants to see the amazing little Welshman:

'My Lords! Gentlemen! The bout for the World Featherweight Championship! Weighing seven stone ten pounds, Featherweight Champion of Great Britain! European Champion! And the World Featherweight Champion! From Tylorstown, Glamorganshire – Jimmy Wilde!'

And there's the Zulu Kid from America in the other corner. He's shorter than Jimmy Wilde, five feet, but strong, stocky. He's very confident. And America acclaims him as the true champion.

The afternoon's event will decide. The two are ready. The first round and the Kid is keeping close to Jimmy. Punches to the stomach. But Jimmy's arms are never-ending, like long knives. Jimmy dancing and the kid looking clumsy. Round Two, and Jimmy hits the stomach and the head. The Kid hits the canvas. A count starts but the bell saves him.

Eighteen more rounds according to the programme. Round Three and Jimmy is as hard as ever. He was working in a pit in the Rhondda at the age of nine. Jimmy's fists are an insane kaleidoscope. The Kid is stubborn and hard. Round Six... Round Nine. And the Kid is pressing the Welshman's ribs. But he's sluggish. And Jimmy is mercurial.

Round Eleven and the thousands inside the Stadium foresee the inevitable. To the left, to the right, up and down. And Jimmy improving with every round. The long steel arms. Hitting, spearing, flowing and hitting again.

The Kid is on the canvas. The hurrahs rise in chords from bench to bench, from row to row, from floor to ceiling. The Kid looks pitiful, his confidence in the spit bucket. And Jimmy leaves the ring as lightfootedly as he had entered. Teddy Lewis had no reason to open his little bag once during the bout.

Jimmy Wilde was the greatest featherweight champion ever. He was world champion for more years than anyone else. He struck more men to the ground than any other featherweight boxer. Between 1910 and 1923 Wilde fought 175 official bouts. He fought with punishing regularity. In September 1913, for example, he fought five times officially. And between these formal events he used to fight in fairs, big and small. He probably fought more than 700 bouts of this kind during his career. And often his opponents were much heavier than him.

Things slowed down after the Great War. In February 1921 he fought officially for the last time in Wales. That was little less than a year before he was beaten by Pancho Villa in New York. Jimmy Wilde died in Cardiff on 10 March 1969.

R. Maldwyn Thomas

BLEDDYN WILLIAMS

Bleddyn Llewellyn Williams is one of the immortals of rugby union, widely recognised as the prince of centres, hailed by South Africans and Kiwis alike as the greatest player in his position of his era. If anything, he was admired more beyond Wales than within it, where it was felt, outside Cardiff, that he never fully showed for Wales the form he constantly attained with his club. There was an element of truth in this, and his international career, though extending from 1947 to 1955, was punctuated by a series of niggling injuries, none serious or prolonged, but frequent enough to limit his number of caps to twenty-two out of a possible forty.

He was born in Taff's Well, north of Cardiff, in 1923, into a large rugby-playing family: the eight Williams brothers all wore Cardiff's blue-and-black over a period extending from 1934 to 1973, a record unlikely to be matched.

Bleddyn Williams leading out the Lions against New Zeland, 1950.

After winning an under-15 schoolboys cap, he caught the eye of Wilfred Wooller, who was instrumental in persuading the headmaster of Rydal School, his own alma mater, to offer a scholarship to the gifted youngster. There on the north Wales coast, he blossomed as a fly-half, and it was in that position that he won his first senior cap against England in 1947. During the wartime international matches, however, W. T. H. Davies's brilliance at outside-half had pushed Bleddyn into the centre, where he flourished. The Service Internationals relaxed the prohibition on amateurs mixing with professionals, and the experience of playing alongside the rich talents of Davies, Gus Risman, and Alan Edwards of the rugby league imbued Bleddyn with a love of the fast-attacking game which he himself came to personify.

With the coming of peace, a sports-starved population thronged to Britain's football grounds to see regular fixtures resumed, and Cardiff RFC entered a golden era. With Haydn Tanner, Billy Cleaver, Jack Matthews and Bleddyn himself the brightest star in this galaxy, Cardiff won 140 out of 166 games between 1945 and 1949. Bleddyn scored 30 tries in his first post-war season and 41 in 1947/48, a record that survived almost fifty years.

At international level, Bleddyn enjoyed particular success against Scotland, piercing the Murrayfield defence with his electrifying jink to score stunning tries there in 1947 and 1949, and another two in 1953, when he was captain. At five foot ten and thirteen stone, Bleddyn was powerfully built and strong in the tackle. But what distinguished him above all else was his attacking prowess, his peerless distribution of the ball, his mastery of the grub-kick for the wing to run on to (and score), and his tactical appreciation. Allied to the calm authority and unruffled composure he conveyed as captain – Wales never lost under Bleddyn's leadership – these qualities enabled him to captain the 1950 Lions in three tests in New Zealand and Australia and lead both Cardiff and Wales to historic victories, the last, to date, by either side, against the All Blacks in 1953. Even in defeat, Bleddyn's stiletto sidesteps defied the stoutest defence, as in Belfast in 1948 and the brilliantly executed scissors movement with Malcolm Thomas that brought a late try against the 1951 Springboks.

Graceful under pressure, resolute in the tackle, lethal in attack, Bleddyn Williams, with his debonair appearance and scrupulously fair and unselfish play, brought to traditional amateur values an emphasis on the pursuit of victory as a legitimate and worthy objective. Defeat should be honourable, but it is victory that should be striven for, and cherished.

Gareth Williams

FREDDIE WILLIAMS

Champion, victor, winner! I suppose the majority of us, at some stage in our lives, have experienced the magic, the thrill, the adrenalin rush when crossing the finishing line, leaving others trailing in our wake. The County's Athletics Championships perhaps, the Egg and Spoon Race at Nursery School, victorious at the area's seven-a-side competition, bravely keeping out a wicked shot to claim the Shield at the National Hockey event, even crossing the chequered flag at Llandow or Pembrey, county champions, national champions, European champions, with celebrations continuing long into the night.

But just consider the following. Imagine the feeling, the honour of being crowned World Champion. Several of us can dream occasionally and perform wondrous deeds at Wimbledon, Wembley or even our very own Millennium Stadium. That tasty piece of Brie or Caerphilly can conjure up various fantasies; tries, goals, runs chalked up before our very eyes! Unfortunately, more often than not, the dreams turn out to be false dawns; hopes turned to ashes!

Not so, as far as Freddie Williams was concerned. Influenced by his father, Fred Williams, the speedway rider from Port Talbot turned pumpkins into coaches in the early fifties and was crowned World Speedway Champion in 1950 and 1953.

Motor bikes were the lifeblood of the Williams family, and the fields around Margam echoed to the screeching sounds of engines. The local inhabitants marvelled at the skill of young Freddie as he succeeded with grim tenacity in piloting his machine in the shadows of the Orangery and the Abbey.

He soon competed in grass track racing and as a member of the Neath Motor Club, developed into an extremely talented and competent racer. As a young apprentice at Portsmouth Dock, Freddie Williams's life was changed dramatically. Speedway racing had been an important part of the British sporting scene and out of the blue, Sir Arthur Elvin, the owner of Wembley Stadium, grabbed the limelight by announcing a scheme to re-open the venue and to finance a team composing solely of British riders.

Some ridiculed the idea. Sir Arthur Elvin advertised for twelve riders in the magazine *Motor Cycling*, appointed Eric Jackson of Bellevue as team manager, and convinced the British public that the scheme could be a successful one.

As far as Freddie Williams was concerned, it was an opportunity of a lifetime. To be successful in the sport one had to win races; it was the only way of

Freddie Williams (centre) – World Champion.

repaying the owners for the loan of the bikes used. Williams responded spectacularly to the challenge, proving himself to be a world-class rider, superior over an eight year career to the stars from Scandinavia, New Zealand, Australia and the United States.

Sir Arthur's vision was truly realised, the Wembley team proved world class and in Freddie Williams they had an outstanding world champion.

Brendan Owen

J. J. WILLIAMS

I was fourteen years of age when I first saw J. J. Williams play. The game was on the Arms Park in 1967, and my Cardigan Grammar School friend Barry Griffiths and I had sneaked away from a very intense Athletic course at Cyncoed to see the Welsh Schools Under-18 team play England. There were two players by the name of Williams who caught the eye in a Welsh victory. One was J. P. R. of Millfield School playing at 15, and the other was J. J. of Maesteg Comprehensive School playing at outside-half. It was the respective courage and pace demonstrated by these two that created the attention. These ingredients proved to be their trade mark as they went on to make rugby history. I was pleased on two counts – one because it was my first visit to the Arms Park and secondly because I myself was a Williams!

It was not a coincidence that the ability of these two blossomed in other sports; J. J. with his athletic achievements and J. P. R. on the tennis courts. His first-class rugby career started at Maesteg and Cardiff Training College, and he then played 100 games for Bridgend between 1970 and 1973, scoring 99 tries.

Whilst it was clear to all that J. J. was going to play a significant role in Welsh rugby, there was no taking anything for granted in the 70s, as there were too many quality players available in each position. This, of course, was the real reason for the successs of that period, as there was so much strength in depth. Even J. J. had to be blessed with some luck in that impressive era. The great John Bevan (younger than J. J.) of Cardiff, Wales and British Lions had to join Warrington Rugby League Club before the Bridgend flyer was given the platform to parade his range of skills.

The fastest wing in the world at the time moved to Llanelli in 1972 and worked under Carwyn James. The success of this period is well documented, and was highlighted by the Scarlets' victory against the All Blacks, a victory in which J. J. played a full part. He put in several effective tackles when the All Black forwards drove down the blind side, and he chased all of Phil Bennett's kicks, putting the opposition under pressure regularly, and forcing defensive mistakes.

It was perhaps on the Lions tour in 1974 that he fully launched his career and embedded his reputation on a worldwide scale. He must have felt that he was back on the running track when he was gliding over the grounds of South Africa. He became the complete finisher on that tour and his record number of tries in a Test Match and consequently the Test Series was an outstanding contribution. His extremely well-placed and deft kicks beyond the opposition defensive line were a joy to behold, and his skill in picking up rolling balls was widely admired – now do you believe that he was initially an outside-half?

He also scored a memorable try in the second test on the British Lions Tour to New Zealand in 1977 and, remarkably, he was just as effective on the muddy grounds of North and South Islands as he had been on the high veldt of South Africa. He returned from the All Black Tour not only having enhanced his playing reputation, but also having advanced his good name as a strong and dedicated personality committed to succeed as an individual and as a member of the team.

Despite his effectiveness as a game breaker there are two particular instances which I recall that took my breath away when playing with and watching John play. They were truly two outstanding passes; one to Phil Bennett in 1977 against France, and the other against England to Paul Ringer. The transfers were executed at real pace and under extreme pressure. To the ordinary mortals amongst us this would not have been an option, but John's awareness, unselfishness and vision led to two great tries. He was a constant danger not only as a try-scorer but also as a try-maker. J. J. Williams, whether in full flight on the track or along the touch-line was always a delight to watch.

Brynmor Williams

J. P. R. WILLIAMS

Full-backs used to be elegant: they sent long kicks, with right foot or left, screwing miles down the touch-lines. Terry Davies of Llanelli, more than any other Welsh full-back, demonstrated the artistry of the catch, the poise and the eye-hand-foot coordination. But then came J. P. R.

He arrived in international rugby in 1969; at the same time as a new law, in fact, which stopped those classy full-backs kicking direct to touch as soon as they had put a foot outside the defensive 25-yard line. I was a rugby writer by this time, and I saw the old images blown apart. Even as I watched John Peter Rhys Williams emerge with London Welsh and Wales, I knew I was watching full-back play being brilliantly rewritten. By the time he had played 55 internationals, and been on two British Lions tours, everyone knew that he would be remembered eventually as the father of modern full-back play.

The running full-back became familiar, but J. P. R. offered more, much more. Timing and strength, a decent sidestep, useful place-kicking and a defence so aggressive that one of his tackles could get the whole of Cardiff Arms Park roaring. Under high kicks, left alone in space, bombarded by the opposition, he could take them on physically, and stay on his feet until support had arrived. I remember his tackle on the French right wing Roger Bourgarel in the Grand Slam match of 1971 in Paris. Better still, I recall Bourgarel sprinting towards the

Welsh line minutes later but this time choosing not to take on J. P. R. He passed, J. P. R. intercepted and off he went up-field to find Gareth Edwards miraculously in support to score a crucial try.

J. P. R. Williams was a bundle of competitive, hard-boned skill, whose need for a high level of physical involvement in play was married to the ability to understand the bigger picture and to behave creatively at all times. He was a truly great rugby player who ached to win and usually did. I am glad he was on our side.

Tony Lewis

MARK WILLIAMS

What is it about the sport of snooker that makes it so strangely compulsive, that it makes millions – a large percentage of them Welsh – stay up until the early hours, rooted to their armchairs with tension – as they did on the night of May 1st, 2000? Is it the element of fallibility, the possibility of a fluke turning the world upside down? Is it the personalities, or the undying belief that the underdog can upset the odds? In the case of Mark Williams and Matthew Stevens – for they will forever be interlinked by that final – there were a number of elements, not least the fact that it was the first ever Welsh final. Wales was the only guaranteed winner that night, but the match had everything, and after defeat at the same stage a year before, few would begrudge Mark Williams much of anything, such is the personality of the man.

His own heroes were Jimmy White and Steve Davis, role models in very different ways. He doesn't remember the time when Llanelli's Terry Griffiths seemingly came from nowhere to become world champion back in 1979.

I do; having grown up with the idea that Llanelli was the centre of the universe, I suddenly had it confirmed, much as the people of Cwm have now, by a mild-mannered, soft spoken Welshman who won hearts wherever he went. What I didn't understand then was what exactly Terry Griffiths's success, along with that of Ray Reardon, Doug Mountjoy and the rest meant for a small country like Wales. Sportsmen are obvious, if sometimes unknowing, ambassadors for their communities and their countries. It's a legacy Mark Williams carries with ease, and one which the whole of Wales can celebrate.

Rhodri Davies

R. H. WILLIAMS

It takes courage for a man from Cwmtwrch to write a 300-word appreciation regarding a rugby player born and bred in Cwmllynfell. The two villages are just a goal-kick apart on the winding road which follows the old LMS railway line from Ystalyfera to Brynaman. To be honest, but for the Berrington Hill, the two villages would be joined at the hip!

There has always been a rivalry between villages in the Swansea, Amman and Neath Valleys, and Cwmllynfell and Cwmtwrch are no exception. Ray Gravell might say, 'West is Best', but personally speaking it's always the Cwmtwrch result which is uppermost in my mind before I even consider Pontypool or Swansea! The rivalry for the most part is a friendly one; an element of suspicion combined with humour, jealousy and stubbornness. The norm is to disagree; arguments are common when one discusses the intricacies of the oval ball. If one praises Shane Williams, the other will extol the virtues of Mark Jones. And when the two sides meet at Cae'r Bryn or Cae Cwm a competent referee and a fair amount of patience and understanding is required.

Rhys Haydn Williams was born in Cwmllynfell, and let's say it and get it out of the way, Cwmllynfell must be credited with the development of one of the true greats in world rugby. The second-row forward was described by a true 'giant' in the rugby world, Colin Meads, as a 'colossus'. His performances during the British Lions Tour of New Zealand in 1959 were really awesome. Colin Meads and Tiny White don't talk all that often but I must quote them: '*If R. H. Williams had been born in New Zealand, he would have played regularly for the All Blacks.*' Rhys was the backbone of The Lions teams who toured South Africa in

1955, and New Zealand and Australia in 1959. He was as hard as teak, a fitness freak and worth his weight in gold in the bowels of a scrummage or in the pandemonium which prevailed at a line-out.

He was also a gifted scholar, a talented pupil at Ystalyfera Grammar School, held a degree from the University of Wales, Aberystwyth, and had a successful career in academia. But rugby was his great love; he possessed an astute mind and was a great thinker on the game's tactics. As a selector, he was always reminding us of the importance of providing good, quick ball to us ballet dancers and his contribution within the four walls of the Committee Room always proved invaluable.

R. H. had this great presence on the rugby field. He was immensely strong and had the ability to withstand pressure to the bitter end. His 'never say die' attitude was an example to all; he would have been an inspiration at Waterloo and Trafalgar.

Clive Rowlands

HOWARD WINSTONE

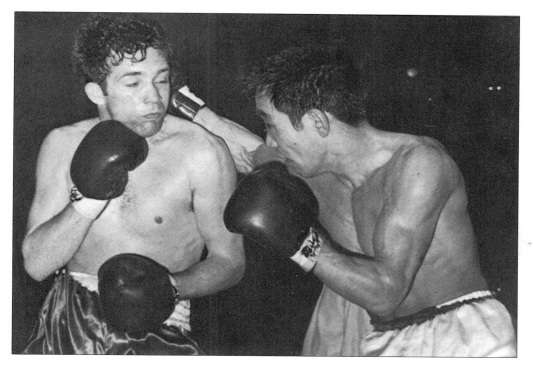

In the 1960s, Carmarthen Market Hall was one of Britain's major boxing venues, and as a young boy I had the privilege of watching great boxers in the ring such as Brian Curvis, Billy Walker, Johnny Prescott, and Lennie 'The Lion' Williams. But my hero, was, and still is, Howard Winstone.

I first saw him defend his European crown in Carmarthen, when his manager Eddie Thomas took the microphone in the centre of the ring and led the crowd singing the national anthem. That fight was broadcast live on BBC and Harry Carpenter was commentating. I still have Harry's autograph somewhere !

But my everlasting memory of Howard's career was not the night he eventually won the world title, but the night of that epic battle against Mexico's Vincente Saldivar at Ninian Park. The date is firmly etched in my memory – January 15, 1967.

We were listening to the fight on the radio in my uncle's car in the Priory Street car park – although that memory is vivid, I cannot remember why we had to listen in the car! According to the men, Howard was ahead on points going into the last round. The rest, as they say, is history. The two gladiators, the commentator was telling us, were toe to toe in the centre of the ring trading punch for punch. I swear that my uncle threw every punch that Howard threw that night. My dream as well as Howard's was shattered when the referee awarded the fight – wrongly according to everyone who saw the fight – to Saldivar.

In January 1968, Howard and manager Eddie Thomas chose Carmarthen as their training base in the build-up to the world title fight against Japan's Mitsunori Seki. They stayed in the Nelson Hotel (alas no longer there) with Griff James, and trained in the gym at the old Carmarthen Quins Club in Nott Square (also sadly gone).

Every night, after my own rugby training, I was in that gym watching Howard being put through his paces, in awe that such a small man could take so much punishment.

January 23, 1968, is carved in my memory. It was the night on which Howard Winstone became World Featherweight Boxing Champion. After nine bruising rounds, the referee stopped the fight in Howard's favour due to Seki's badly cut eye.

He was champion for just six months but that was long enough for me. He lost his title to Jose Legra of Cuba in front of his home crowd in Porthcawl on July 24.

It was 25 years later, in 1993, that I had the pleasure of meeting Howard Winstone for the first time. A couple of us researchers on the S4C *Heno* production team were boxing fans, and were following Cardiff's Steve Robinson's challenge for the title against John Davison in the North East. Steve had come from nowhere to win the world crown, and it came to light that his hero too, was Howard Winstone and that the pair had never met.

Steve and his manager Dai Gardiner came to the studio in Swansea, with the championship belt, and Howard was only too pleased to be contacted and came down to meet the new champion. I was in the company of not one but two world champions, and it truly was my pleasure to buy the first round when we retired to the New York public house for a drink after the programme.

Adrian Howells

MARTIN WOODROFFE

'Fancy going to the 'baars' on Saturday?'

For the uninitiated, the 'baars' was Cardiffian dialect for 'The Swimming Baths'. As an eight-year-old growing up in Cardiff in the late 60s, such a jaunt entailed rolling a pair of hand-knitted woollen bathing trunks cylindrically inside a minute towel, extorting half a crown (12p) from my father, and catching a number 17 from Ely to the Central Bus Station. From there it was but a short, gleeful jog to that famous landmark hugging the banks of the River Taff and the scene of a thousand childhood pilgrimages – The Wales Empire Pool.

So why visit a swimming pool where the legendary coolness of the water could induce hypothermia in a polar bear, whilst simultaneously inflicting several varieties of verruca on unsuspecting patrons, when for the same financial outlay a sport-mad youngster could watch Gareth Edwards strut his stuff at the Arms Park, or admire John Toshack's aerial dominance at Ninian Park – not to mention Tony Lewis's captivating elegance at Sophia Gardens? The answer lay in the exploits of an eighteen-year-old swimmer from Fairwater, Cardiff at the 1968 Mexico City Olympics.

On the morning of Friday, October 25th I sat transfixed as our grainy old 'Rediffusion' black and white television showed 'Uncle' Frank Bough on Olympic Grandstand informing the nation of Martin Woodroffe's achievement the previous evening. A silver medal in the 200 metres butterfly in a time of 2 minutes 9 seconds – merely 0.3 seconds behind gold medal winner Carl Robie of the USA. And he (Woodroffe) actually trained at my Empire Pool – unbelievable!

It was the first ever Olympic swimming medal to be won by a Welshman and how we celebrated! That evening, it seemed that every child in Cardiff descended on 'The Empire'. Not that butterfly is the easiest stroke known to mankind! As I remember, the pool became a boiling cauldron of thrashing limbs and piercing shrieks as we all tried to emulate our hero; four hundred children heaving through the water like arthritic frogs.

I never did master 'butterfly', and regretfully if I swim these days it is in the characterless setting of an excessively warm health club pool, the Empire Pool having been sadly demolished to make way for the Millennium Stadium. But

nothing can erase the memory of those blissful childhood days, crouching with toes curled over the edge of the waterside anticipating the cool, chlorinated shock and challenging a friend, 'Come on, I'll race you. One length, I'll be Martin Woodroffe!'

Phil Steele

WILFRED WOOLLER

In pre-revolutionary days, five years before Gwynfor Evans captured Carmarthen, I knew a boy who believed that if Saunders Lewis and Wilfred Wooller saw fit to join the same Welsh political party, Wales would get self-government within a week, for England could not and would not suffer their soldered resolution.

Wooller was a law unto himself. For a man who had defied Japan in a prisoner of war camp, it didn't take too much courage to bowl underarm against Sussex at Swansea and make Robin Marlar snarl, or summarily to dismiss contracted cricketers for bad shows, either directly, as allegedly happened to Hedges and Pressdee, or indirectly on television, as Wooller often did as a commentator, commenting (it must be remembered) on his own coached charges. He was terrific and he was terrifying.

A newscaster once called him Wolf Willer, a Freudian slip of genius, for that's him, that's it, half-beast half-deity slouching not towards Bethlehem to be born but towards the pavilion at St Helens to pontificate to another committee. Secretary and Captain, one had the sense that he could eat Don Ward for breakfast, but that he much preferred to have him grilled by close fielding.

Hiraeth is yearning to see Wooller and Haydn Davies at the crease together, the one doggedly defensive for the side's sake, the other clatching leather for the fun of it, both with their broad backs bent in defiance and derring-do. I never saw Haydn Davies after he retired. Wilf became omnipresent, an England selector (capital S), with G. V. Wynne-Jones a force of sorts in Welsh Conservative circles, the man who gave us Majid, the Preface writer for the Glamorgan Year Book, a Sunday newspaper columnist, a rugby commentator, and the most conspicuous wearer of mismatched checks in Welsh sartorial history (something Saunders Lewis would not have approved of). Above all, he was Glamorgan personified.

Man of myth, as he would modestly say.

Derec Llwyd Morgan

IAN WOOSNAM

Tickets at the United States Masters are hard to come by. They're usually handed down from generation to generation – the by now familiar plastic card accreditation is required to gain entry into the VIP enclosure and the plush clubhouse. The year following Woosnam's victory at Augusta, Stan Thomas, Ian Botham and yours truly travelled to the US to support our bosom pal. Woosie's constant ability to do the unusual and at times the utterly impossible comes as no surprise, and on this occasion we were the beneficiaries.

His family (who were entitled to special tickets and privileges) decided to stay at home and Ian duly packaged some items originally intended for his wife and daughters. They arrived by courier at our hotel. I should stress that the security at the Augusta National resembles the Arrivals Hall at Tel Aviv and Jerusalem Airports and upon approaching the Main Gate for VIPs we were stopped and interrogated thus:

'ID, Sir?' quizzed an officious looking security guard in a precise and courteous manner (nothing like the stewards at Lord's – in fact, if the said stewards had been positioned along the south coast of England during the last war, Hitler would never have contemplated invading Britain).

I pointed proudly to the plastic card hanging loosely around my neck. I half expected to be allowed entry immediately but I was stopped in my tracks. He continue to question me,

'Is that your name Sir – Amy Woosnam?'

'It is,' I replied with a measure of conviction and embarassment, 'it's a very popular Christian name in South Wales.'

'Can you cofirm, Sir, that you friend's name is Amy Woosnam,' the official asked Stan Thomas who was next in line and breathing heavily.

'I certainly can,' said Stan, who now had to convince our American friend that his name was Rebecca!

But the magical moment was to hear Ian Botham, the most famous cricketer in the world, a man who epitomises male chauvinism at its highest level, a combination of Alexander the Great, Roy of the Rovers and Bruce Willis stating categorically that his name was Glendryth Woosnam! What would Viv Richards and Dennis Lillee have said?

Ian Woosnam's zest for life has not mellowed; he is a much liked individual. The family man from Jersey is immensely popular on the golfing circuit especially in Japan, probably because of his short stature; he could possibly have ended up playing No. 8 for their national rugby team! The blue eyes are merry and candid; the smile warm and mischievous. He always insists that the highlights of his career were the 1991 US Masters victory and his participation at the Max Boyce Classic at Glyn-neath in 1985!

On the golf course his uncanny judgement, his ability to take a stranglehold on the game and his admirable consistency resulted in successes at major tournaments. His timing was as immaculate as a Swiss chronometer, and his metronomic swing has been admired by golf critics worldwide. He certainly boasts the most impressive statistics of any golfer 'from tee to green' but concedes that his wayward putting has let him down of late. Ian Woosnam is a total professional; his preparations are always meticulous as they were for the party held in his honour at Oswestry in 1991 after his Masters triumph. 'I was there', and I can testify to Sam Torrence's non-appearance at Birmingham Airport the following day. As Lee Trevino once said, 'They'll never bury Woosie because they'll never get his heart into the coffin!'

To be truly great you have to have total belief in your own excellence – that about sums up Ian Woosnam.

Max Boyce

TERRY YORATH

Tragedy and disaster are two of the most overused words in sport; in recent years Hillsborough, Bradford and Heysel have left us bereft of adjectives, but it can be said that Terry Yorath has been touched by tragedy and shouldered the burden with a strength of character that is the mark of the man.

Assistant manager at Bradford when 56 people perished, and manager of Wales when his own son Daniel died almost exactly seven years later at the age of 15, Terry Yorath knows that mere defeat cannot truly be called either tragedy or disaster.

Above all, Yorath was a leader of men; never the most elegant of footballers he was the foil that allowed others the freedom to express themselves as Glen Hoddle and Ossie Ardiles will testify. His playing career took him from Leeds to Spurs, Coventry and Vancouver Whitecaps, but it was with Wales that we saw Terry Yorath in his true colours.

59 International caps, 42 of them as captain – his own team mates will tell you that he was never one to hide and would refuse to allow his side to under-perform; he had exacting standards for himself and others, a fact that was to frustrate him continually when managing players at a lower level.

As captain he took Wales to the last eight of the European Championship, and as a manager it was the width of a crossbar that prevented a trip to the World Cup in America. Political infighting brought about his demise: had the word compromise been in his dictionary he wouldn't have been such a good player but he would still be manager of Wales.

John Hardy